VOICES FROM THE MARGINS: MIGRANT WOMEN'S EXPERIENCES IN SOUTHERN AFRICA

KATE LEFKO-EVERETT

SERIES EDITOR:
PROF. JONATHAN CRUSH

SOUTHERN AFRICAN MIGRATION PROJECT
2007

Published by Idasa, 6 Spin Street, Church Square, Cape Town, 8001, and
Southern African Research Centre, Queen's University, Canada.

Copyright Southern African Migration Project (SAMP) 2007
ISBN 1-920118-50-0

First published 2007
Design by Bronwen Müller
Typeset in Goudy

CONTENTS   PAGE

TABLES   PAGE

FIGURES   PAGE

EXECUTIVE SUMMARY

The concept of the feminization of migration traditionally refers to the growth in numbers and relative importance of women's migration, particularly from and within developing countries. In Africa, for example, the proportion of female migrants rose from 42% of the total in 1960 to almost 50% at the present time. This process is a result, first, of the continued impoverishment and marginalization of many women in developing countries; and second, of the increasing demand for female labour in the service industries of industrial and industrializing countries.

The United Nations suggests that the full implications of migration and mobility for women are difficult to assess, due to a dearth of data on women and migration. What also eludes official statistics is the extent to which women migrants are independent actors in migration decision-making. There remains a lack of understanding of women's motives and experiences in the migration process, which is linked historically to the invisibility and marginalization of women as migrants. In Southern Africa, there is still a serious lack of gendered analysis of contemporary cross-border migration, and limited understanding of women's experiences as migrants.

Migration to South Africa in the twentieth century consisted of two main types:

- Immigrants, exclusively white until the mid-1980s, came primarily as "family class" migrants from Europe, with women accompanying their working spouses.
- Migrants, primarily black and male, were allowed temporary entry to South Africa under bilateral agreements with sending states (such as Botswana, Lesotho, Malawi, Mozambique and Swaziland). Although temporary migration was male-dominated, some women did accompany their spouses or left on their own for South Africa.

Since 1990, the number of women migrants to South Africa has increased dramatically, although a recent SAMP survey shows that with the exception of Zimbabwe, temporary migration in the SADC is still male-dominated. Women have become far more mobile but may not be moving primarily as economic migrants who work or are looking for work. Gender roles tend to produce a more varied set of reasons for circular movements among women. Overall, female migrants are generally older and more educated than male migrants, and more likely to be married. Women migrants are motivated by a range of social, economic and reproductive factors, but are less likely to seek formal employment than males. They are more likely to travel for purposes of cross-border trade and are likely to stay for shorter periods and engage less with the formal economy or social networks.

SAMP's Migration and Gender Conference in 2002 determined that there was a need for more in-depth research with a specific focus on women's migration experiences to complement statistical data. SAMP developed the Migrant Voices Project (MVP) in 2004 and, in 2005, conducted an in-depth, qualitative study with women migrants both temporarily and permanently living in South Africa, as well as with South African women who had returned to the country after migrating.

Through these interviews, the MVP gathered qualitative information from women migrants on a range of issues including: migration decision-making, travel preparations, experiences while migrating, resulting in household and lifestyle changes, experiences of living in a foreign country, and treatment from family and community when returning to countries of origin. Beyond personal experiences, the MVP also explored women's perceptions of the importance of migration in the Southern African Development Community (SADC) region, reasons for women's migration in particular, awareness of policy, and gender-specific challenges encountered. Finally, SAMP aimed to glean policy recommendations from women migrants themselves, against a backdrop of the re-drafting of immigration regulations in South Africa, and renewed uptake of the SADC Facilitation of Movement Protocol.

The findings of the MVP are presented in considerable depth in this paper. They confirm some aspects of our previous understanding of why women migrate: for many, migration is a survival strategy driven primarily by household need. Migration also allows women the opportunity to work, to earn their own money and to exercise greater decision-making power in their daily lives. However, the MVP also challenged current understanding in a number of respects. Many of the migrant women interviewed are independent agents in migration decision-making, rather than deferring to male partners or parents, and have defied resistance from families and communities. Some challenge the idea that migration is motivated purely by economic and livelihood needs, instead valuing the fundamental experience of travel in itself, and the personal benefit of exposure to other cultures, languages and ideas. In terms of gendered migration experiences, many women feel male migrants are as vulnerable, if not more so than women, for a number of complex reasons. Although many travel to South Africa through irregular means, they place high value on the right of governments to control and manage migration, and wish to regularize their own status. And, though knowledge of migration policy and regulations differs, women articulated a number of key migration policy recommendations for the region.

This publication, as well as drawing conclusions from women's descriptions of their experiences as migrants, also provides a forum for the voices of women themselves to be heard. Providing a means for those voices to be heard by policy-makers and others in positions of power is always a challenge. SAMP's Migration Policy Series is widely consulted by those who make the rules. By providing space for women to speak (through copious verbatim reproduction of their comments), SAMP anticipates that these voices will be heard and will affect the current policy debate. Migration conferences, workshops and forums are notable in Southern Africa for the absence of migrants themselves. SAMP hopes that this publication will prompt greater policy attention to the voices, needs and experiences of ordinary women.

Introduction

I n recent years migration studies have increasingly focused on the "feminization" of international migration.[1] The concept of feminization has referred to the growth in numbers and relative importance of women's migration in some parts of the world. Migration has traditionally been seen as a primarily male domain, particularly in developing countries. The growth in women's migration is seen to reflect two things: first, the continued impoverishment and marginalization of many women in developing countries, and second, increasing demand for female labour in the service industries of industrial and industrializing countries.

However, on a global scale, Hania Zlotnik has analyzed UN global migration estimates and concludes that women and girls have actually accounted for a very high proportion of all international migrants "for a long time."[2] In 1960, for example, the global migrant stock of 75 million included 35 million females (or 47% of the total). In 2005, there were 94.5 million females in a global stock of 191 million (or 49% of the total).[3] At a global scale, the feminization of migration therefore refers more to absolute increases in the number of female migrants rather than any dramatic shift in the relative proportions of male versus female migration.

When developed and developing countries are compared, a slightly different picture emerges (Table 1). The number of female migrants in developed countries increased from 16 million to 60 million between 1960 and 2005. The growth in developing countries was much smaller, though still substantial (from 20 million to 34 million). The proportion of female migrants in developed countries increased marginally from 49% in 1960 to 52% in 2005. In contrast, in developing countries the proportion was virtually the same in 1960 and 2005 (at around 45%). The African story is rather different. In the continent as a whole, the proportion of female migrants rose from 42% to 47% between 1960 and 2005. Table 2 shows a proportional decline in the share of female migration in Northern Africa (down from 50% to 43%) but increases in Western Africa (42% to 49%), Middle or Central Africa (44% to 46%), Eastern Africa (42% to 48%) and Southern Africa (30% to 42%). In all areas, and Southern Africa in particular, male migration still far surpasses female migration. But with the exception of North Africa, the absolute and relative importance of female migration has increased.[4]

Table 1: Global Migration Stock of Migrants 1960-2005						
	Millions					
	1960	1970	1980	1990	2000	2005
World	75.46	81.34	99.28	154.95	176.74	190.63
Male	40.14	42.91	52.39	78.98	88.98	96.11
Female	35.33	38.43	46.88	75.97	87.76	94.51
Developed countries	32.31	38.36	47.48	82.37	105.00	115.40
Male	16.53	19.61	23.80	39.57	50.28	55.19
Female	15.79	18.75	23.65	42.80	54.73	60.26
Developing countries	43.15	42.97	51.82	72.58	71.73	75.24
Male	23.61	23.30	29.59	39.41	38.70	40.98
Female	19.54	19.68	23.23	33.17	33.03	34.26

Source: UNDP, Trends in Total Migrant Stock: The 2005 Revision (Online Data base)

Table 2: Proportional Gender Breakdown of Global Migration Stock by Region 1960-2005						
Major area	1960	1970	1980	1990	2000	2005
World	46.8	47.2	47.2	49.0	49.7	49.6
More developed regions	48.9	48.9	49.8	52.0	52.1	52.2
Less developed regions	45.3	45.8	44.8	45.7	46.1	45.5
Europe	48.4	47.7	48.1	52.8	53.4	53.4
Northern America	50.5	51.5	52.6	51.0	50.4	50.4
Oceania	44.4	46.5	47.9	49.1	50.6	51.3
Africa	42.3	42.7	44.1	45.9	47.2	47.4
Northern Africa	49.5	47.7	45.8	45.6	44.4	43.6
Southern Africa	30.1	30.3	35.6	38.7	41.3	42.4
Western Africa	42.1	43.0	43.5	46.4	48.8	49.0
Middle Africa	44.0	45.5	45.9	46.0	46.2	46.3
Eastern Africa	41.9	43.2	45.3	47.3	47.9	48.3
Asia	46.4	46.8	44.6	45.2	45.4	44.7
Eastern Asia	47.4	48.6	46.8	49.1	52.8	53.5
Southeastern Asia	45.4	46.9	46.1	46.1	47.6	48.6
Western Asia	46.9	44.9	40.7	39.9	40.1	38.8
Latin America and Caribbean	44.7	46.8	48.2	49.7	50.2	50.3
Central America	47.7	49.8	49.8	50.5	49.6	49.5
South America	44.4	46.6	48.3	49.8	50.6	50.8
Caribbean	45.3	46.1	46.5	47.7	49.0	49.4

The feminization of migration is also increasingly viewed as involving a qualitative change in women's movements. More and more women are migrating for work in their own right, particularly within the developing world. Feminization therefore implies a change in migratory roles from women being dependents of male migrants to being autonomous economic migrants. Graeme Hugo argues: "There has been a substantial increase in the involvement of women in international circular labour migration. This is evident in the increasing numbers of women moving as international students and being recruited into high-level, high-skill managerial, executive, and professional jobs. In [many countries], the greatest involvement of women is in the lower end of the labour market."[5]

The United Nations Division for the Advancement of Women suggests that the "full implications of migration and mobility for women" are "difficult to assess," due primarily to a "dearth of data on women and migration" linked to inconsistency in the availability, quality and comparability of international migration statistics, particularly originating from government sources.[6] What also eludes official UN statistics is the extent to which women migrants are, to use Robin Cohen's words, the "baggage of male workers" or if they are in fact independent actors in migration decision-making.[7] There remains a lack of understanding of women's motives and experiences in the migration process, which according to Monica Boyd and Elizabeth Grieco, is linked historically to the "near invisibility of women as migrants, their presumed passivity in the migration process, and their assumed place in the home."[8]

In Southern Africa, Belinda Dodson and Jonathan Crush link this to a bias associated with the "long association of labour migration with the mining sector" and suggest that:

> The power of the regional labour migration paradigm, with its androcentric, 'kraal to compound' logic, has been put forward as one of the main explanations for the neglect of women in Southern African migration studies, except as those 'left behind.' As Barnes argues, this has produced 'a normative illusion which has practically become conventional wisdom: Africa women were "passive rural widows" who stayed put somewhere, practicing subsistence, and later, cash crop agricultural production while their men departed, perhaps never to return.[9]

Although there are important exceptions in work by historians and historical geographers on past internal and international women's migration, there has been a lack of gendered analysis of contemporary cross-border migration, and limited understanding of womens' agency in the present.[10]

GENDERED PATTERNS OF MIGRATION TO SOUTH AFRICA

M igration to South Africa in the twentieth century consisted of two
main types:

- Immigrants, exclusively white until the mid-1980s, came primarily
as "family class" migrants from Europe, with women accompanying their working spouses. The result was reasonably close gender
parity in the new migrant stock of the country from the 1940s
through to the early 1980s (Figure 1). Thereafter, although the
absolute numbers of male and female immigrants declined dramatically, gender parity was maintained.
- Migrants, primarily black and male, were allowed temporary
entry to South Africa under bilateral agreements with sending
states (such as Botswana, Lesotho, Malawi, Mozambique and
Swaziland). Migrants were employed in industries like mining.
Undocumented migrants were often coerced into working on
white farms.[11] Patriarchal forces tended to immobilize women in
the rural areas of those countries from which male migrants were
recruited in large numbers.[12]

Figure 1: Immigrants by Gender 1950-2003, South Africa

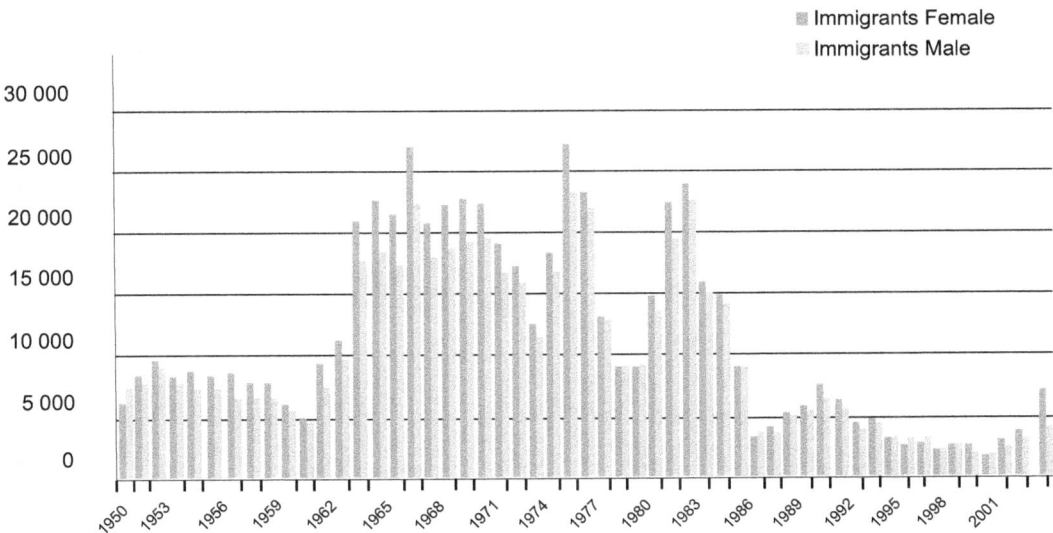

Source: StatsSA Documented Migration, 2003.

Although temporary migration was always male-dominated, some
women did accompany their spouses or left on their own for South Africa
where they worked in beer brewing, cooking, laundry and commercial
sex.[13] Tighter restrictions were introduced by the apartheid state in the

7

1950s and the influx of women was stayed. Many were also forcibly sent home. However, as Figure 2 shows, temporary migration of women to South Africa did continue, although not in the same volume as male migration. Unfortunately gendered data for the 1990s is unavailable, but all evidence suggests that there has been a significant increase in temporary female migration to South Africa. Dodson and Crush note that "the apparent increase in women's migration to South Africa over the 1990s thus perhaps represents more of a return to a pattern that prevailed in the first half of the twentieth century than anything entirely new."[14]

Figure 2: Arrivals by Gender 1963-1992, South Africa

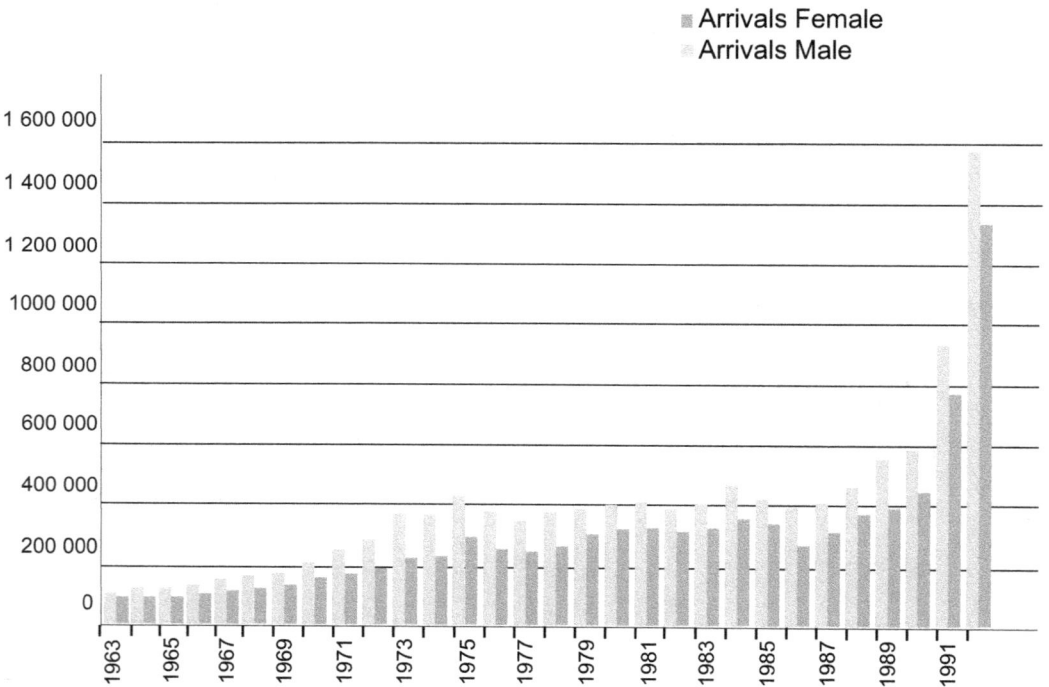

Source: StatsSA Tourism Report, 2003.

Recent data from SAMP's Migration and Remittances Survey (MARS) provides a contemporary snapshot of the gender makeup of labour migration within the SADC region.[15] The survey was carried out in five countries (Botswana, Lesotho, Mozambique, Swaziland and Zimbabwe) and generated detailed data on 4700 migrants. The data will be analyzed in depth from a gender perspective in a forthcoming SAMP policy series paper. However, as Table 3 shows, the economic migration stream from these five countries is still heavily male-dominated. Only in the Zimbabwean case, with 56% of migrant's male and 44% female, is there anything approaching parity in the migration of men and women. In all of the other countries, female migrants are still a small minority, despite evidence that women are becoming far more mobile than they were. Internal migration, however, shows a very different picture with women migrating from rural to urban areas in similar numbers as men.

Table 3: Migration to South Africa by Gender, 2004		
	% Male	% Female
Botswana	95	5
Lesotho	84	16
Mozambique	94	6
Swaziland	92	8
Zimbabwe	56	44
Total	86	14
Source: SAMP MARS		

Women have become far more mobile but may not be moving primarily as economic migrants who work or are looking for work. This hypothesis tends to be supported by SAMP's gender-based analyses of migration data collected in Lesotho, Zimbabwe and Mozambique in the late 1990s. Dodson's analysis of this data has shown how gender roles tend to produce a more varied set of reasons for circular movements among women.[16] She identifies a number of key characteristics amongst the women migrants sampled: overall, female migrants were generally older and more educated than male migrants, and more likely to be married. Women migrants were motivated by a range of social, economic and reproductive factors, but were less likely to seek formal employment than males (Table 4). Women migrants were more likely to travel for purposes of cross-border trade, meaning that they sought urban destinations with opportunities for trade and shopping, and were likely to stay for shorter periods and engage less with the formal economy or social networks. Critically, Dodson also found that women were "less likely to migrate independently" and "more likely to be subject to the will of a (male) parent or partner," and were more likely than men to view their personal migration experiences as "negative" overall.

Table 4: Gender Differences in Migration to South Africa, 1997		
Purpose of Most Recent Visit to SA	Males (%)	Females (%)
Work	33	7
Look for work	17	3
Business	3	3
Buy and sell goods	4	10
Shopping	13	23
Visit family/friends	17	38
Holiday	3	3
Medical	2	8
Other	8	5
Source: SAMP data base		

However, few studies in Southern Africa have concentrated directly on how, and why, women make the decision to migrate, perhaps due to their "presumed passivity in the migration process."[17] Dodson's analysis indicated that 65% of women sampled "said that if they were to migrate, the decision would be taken for them by someone other than themselves," and 49% said that their family would "discourage" or "strongly discourage" them from going.[18] How, then, do women in the region come to reach migration decisions? How independent are they in making migration decisions, and how have members of their families and communities responded?

SAMP's Migration and Gender Conference in 2002 determined that there was a need for more in-depth research with a specific focus on women's migration experiences to complement and add nuance to existing statistical data and profiles. As part of a broader research and policy module on Migration and Gender, SAMP developed the Migrant Voices Project (MVP) at a workshop in Botswana in 2004. In 2005, SAMP conducted an in-depth, qualitative study with women migrants both temporarily and permanently living in South Africa, as well as with South African women who had returned to the country after migrating.

Through these interviews, the MVP gathered qualitative information from women migrants on a range of issues including: migration decision-making, travel preparations, experiences while migrating, household and lifestyle changes, experiences of living in a foreign country, and treatment from family and community when returning to countries of origin. Beyond personal experiences, the MVP also explored women's perceptions of the importance of migration in the Southern African Development Community (SADC) region, reasons for women's migration in particular, awareness of policy, and gender-specific challenges encountered. Finally, SAMP aimed to glean policy recommendations from women migrants themselves, against a backdrop of the re-drafting of immigration regulations in South Africa, and renewed uptake of the SADC Facilitation of Movement Protocol.[19]

The findings of the MVP confirm some aspects of our previous understanding of why women migrate: for many, migration was a survival strategy driven primarily by household need. As observed by Dodson, women participants tended to migrate in "response to difficult circumstances" in countries of origin, while maintaining strong ties with family and home.[20] Migration also, as recognized by the Global Commission on Migration (GCIM), allowed women the opportunity "to work, to earn their own money and to exercise greater decision-making power in their daily lives."[21]

However, the MVP also challenged current theory and understanding in a number of respects. Many of the migrant women were independent agents in migration decision-making, rather than deferring to male partners or parents, and had defied resistance from families and communities. Some participants also challenged the idea that migration was motivated purely by economic and livelihood needs, instead valuing the fundamental experience of travel in itself, and the personal benefit of exposure to other cultures, languages and ideas. In terms of gendered migration experiences, many women felt male migrants were as vulnerable, if not more so than women, for a number of complex reasons. Although many had travelled to South Africa through irregular means, participants placed high value on the right of governments to control and manage migration, and wished to regularize their own status. And, though knowledge of migration policy and regulations differed amongst participants, women articulated a number of key migration policy recommendations for the region.

RESEARCH METHODS

Recognizing the enormous diversity of women migrants in the region, and the breadth of difference in their experiences, the MVP sought to interview participants from a variety of migrant categories:

- *Long-term female migrants*, defined as non-South Africans who had sought to establish themselves in South Africa through work, study, marriage or partnership, or immigration, and planned to stay in the country for no less than six months;
- *Short-term female migrants*, defined as non-South Africans temporarily visiting South Africa for purposes other than a holiday or long-term establishment (the majority of these participants were cross-border traders);

- *Returned female migrants*, defined as South Africans who had experience living in another country for purposes other than a holiday;
- *Male informants* with specific insight into women's migration, including partners and family members of women migrants.

Separate interview guides were developed for each category of participant. In total, in-depth interviews were conducted with 34 long-term, 16 short-term, and 9 returned migrants, as well as 10 male informants. All of the interviews were conducted in the Johannesburg area, and lasted between 20-90 minutes. Refugees and asylum-seekers were specifically excluded from the research, but migrants who had entered the country through irregular, as well as regular, means were included.

As a supplement to the in-depth interviews, six Focus Groups (FGs) were conducted: four in Yeoville, Johannesburg and two in Makhado (formerly Louis Trichardt) close to the border between Limpopo Province and Zimbabwe. All Focus Group participants were also asked to draw a picture or map of their migration experience, which formed the basis of much discussion and debate that took place, and has been used as qualitative data in addition to the spoken texts analysed in this paper.

While the research generated an enormously rich data set, a number of methodological limitations merit mention, primarily related to the relative homogeneity of the sample. First, SAMP aimed to identify research participants from across the SADC region, but Zimbabwean women (24) were heavily represented in comparison with women from Botswana (3), Lesotho (7), Malawi (5), Mozambique (5), Namibia (1), Swaziland (4) and Zambia (1). Given the relative importance of female migration from Zimbabwe, this is less of a problem than it might otherwise have been. Second, it was difficult for the fieldworkers to identify less "visible" female labour migrants in Johannesburg and, as a result, many of both the short- and long-term migrants are market vendors and traders. Fieldworkers also struggled to identify returned migrants who fitted the parameters of the study.

Although the research for the MVP was entirely qualitative, some demographic data about participants was collected, which provides a useful point of departure for the data analysis. Table 5 below shows the distribution of the respondents according to country of origin and category of migrant.

Table 5: Participants by Nationality and Migrant Category					
Country of Origin	Short-Term	Long-Term	Returned	Male	Total
Botswana	1	2	0	0	3
Ghana	0	0	0	1	1
Lesotho	3	4	0	0	7
Malawi	2	3	0	0	5
Mozambique	0	5	0	1	6
Namibia	1	0	0	0	1
South Africa	0	0	4	3	7
Swaziland	1	3	0	1	5
Zambia	0	1	0	0	1
Zimbabwe	8	16	0	4	28
Total	16	34	4	10	64

The participants ranged in age from 18-50, with an average age of 29. Returned migrants were younger on average (24) than long-term (28) or short-term (31) migrants. With a relatively young group of participants, 30 of 49 women described their marital status as "single," 14 were married, 2 were divorced and 3 widowed. Of the 49 women who described their families, only 11 did not have any children. Although 60% of the women were single, two thirds of these had one or more children, suggesting that many may have been primary breadwinners. Finally, 43% of the women were traders or vendors, 11% domestic workers, 11% students, 8% hairdressers, while the rest were in a variety of occupations ranging from unskilled pieceworkers to professionals. Eleven percent of the respondents were unemployed at the time of the interview.

Table 6: Participants by Occupation and Migrant Category				
Occupation	Short-Term	Long-Term	Returned	Total
Trader/vendor	13	9	0	22
Domestic worker	0	5	0	5
Unemployed	0	4	1	5
Student	0	3	2	5
Hairdresser	0	4	0	4
Public phone operator	0	2	0	2
Telemarketer	0	1	1	2
Marketing/business	1	0	0	1
Porter	1	0	0	1
Crime watch	1	0	0	1
Secretary	0	0	0	1
Seamstress	0	1	0	1
Piecework/odd jobs	0	1	0	1
Total	16	30	5	51

The respondents all began migrating between 1990 and 2004, coinciding with the dramatic increase in female arrivals in South Africa directly following the transition to democracy. As anticipated, many short-term migrants described frequent travel, often staying in South Africa for up to three months as permitted by visitor's permits, and returning to their countries of origin as often as "every two or three weeks." In contrast, most long-term migrants said that their journey to South Africa was their first migration experience, and many had never returned home. Those who had returned home went once or twice per year, for holidays and special occasions such as weddings and funerals. The long-term migrants in South Africa, as well as the returned migrants, had only travelled to their main destination country. Short-term migrants reported traveling to other countries in the region, including Botswana, Malawi, Mozambique, Namibia, Zambia, Swaziland and Zimbabwe, as well as overseas.

THE DECISION TO MIGRATE

Analysis of the interviews revealed that poverty, hardship and living conditions in countries of origin were the most significant "push factors" that led these women to take the decision to migrate. This is consistent with Dodson and Crush's more general observation that "for both genders, but perhaps especially for women, migration is a means of problem-solving; a strategic response to their social, economic, environmental, political or personal circumstances."[22] The majority of MVP participants named "work" or "job opportunities" as their primary motive in migrating to their country of destination. In a number of cases, pursuit of work and job opportunities in response to household poverty or hardship was also linked to relationship breakdowns and the absence of a male partner or spouse, or less frequently of parents, as main providers and breadwinners. Beyond economic push factors women cited political instability and intolerance, as well as gender inequality as factors in their migration decision-making.

Expectations about destination countries also featured in migration decision-making, and many of the women had anticipated that South Africa in particular would offer them employment opportunities, access to consumer goods and commodities, and a better quality of life than in countries of origin. These perceived incentives motivated women to migrate even when they met with resistance from family and community members who often expressed concerns over the migrants' vulnerability to crime, violence and victimization. As a result, some women ultimately opted to leave home without telling anyone where they were going. Their resolve confirms both the real strength of the push factors discussed in this section, as well as the relative agency and independence of the women interviewed in making their own migration decisions.

Dodson found that amongst many women in Southern Africa, migration was often "a response to difficult circumstances in the home countries."[23] This was confirmed by MVP participants, with women from Lesotho, Malawi, Mozambique, Swaziland, Zambia and Zimbabwe all describing poverty, hardship, and a low quality of life as the main reasons for migrating. For many women, this was simply a case of unemployment or a lack of job opportunities in their home countries. However, others cited scarcity and shortages of food and fuel in particular, high levels of inflation, the rising cost of goods and basic necessities, drought, and poor educational systems and/or inability to pay school fees:

> [The situation in Zimbabwe] is right but the problem is sometimes you can't get some of the things like food and they're hungry. You see, when I come from this side I've got food and clothes for my kids, everything…. When I go home I can't afford to survive. [If I come to South Africa] I can afford to live for a whole month with the money I got here and clothes, so it's better you see (Participant 49).

> The main reason for migration was to find a better life because things back home [in Zambia] were very ugly. There were no jobs, inflation, drought and many other things (Participant 18).

A participant in a Johannesburg FG described similar hardships in Zimbabwe:

> If only [the South African police] knew that in Zimbabwe it's difficult, that's the poorest country in the whole world. It's difficult living in Zimbabwe because you can't get a job nor even sell something, but you just sit there and starve to death, but they harass us a lot…. Life is tough at home, [we] need to survive…. We are not here by accident but by design. If life was fine we would not be here (Focus Group 3, Participant 7).

For a number of women migrants, the impetus of socioeconomic push factors was strengthened by family and relationship breakdowns. Three younger participants linked their decision to migrate to the absence of fathers in their homes, as described by a Mozambican woman:

> I come from Mozambique. I could say that we were poor at home…. We had a father, because he was still alive. I used to tell myself that I didn't have a father, because he didn't take care of us (Focus Group 4, Participant 3).

Another linked her decision to migrate to her mother, stating that in her country of origin, it was "tough" because "there was no one to take care of us" (Participant 30). Other women attributed poverty and harsh living conditions to loss of income from spouses and male partners. In some instances, this occurred with the death of a husband or partner, as in the case of a widow from Swaziland. While she felt "Swaziland is a beautiful country" and "it is nice and free" (Participant 16), she had received no social assistance as a widow, and felt she had no option but to migrate to South Africa to look for work. For most women, loss of income from a male breadwinner was due to a relationship or family breakdown:

> I left Mozambique because I lost my family and I wasn't working. My husband left me; he left me with the kids.... I left Mozambique and came here because there are no jobs. When a husband leaves you and you don't work – things were bad for me (Focus Group 4, Participant 1).

> [The situation in Zimbabwe] was wrong for those of us who are not working because we didn't have jobs, because we depended on our husbands. So I saw that staying here [in Zimbabwe] won't help, I have to go out and make a living for my children because their father has forgotten them and he is no longer supporting them ... the children could end up dying of hunger and so forth (Participant 23).

> My husband has got another wife, he's enjoying with that wife since 1995, and I am suffering with my children (Focus Group 5, Participant 1).

While in these, and a number of other, cases relationship breakdowns were ultimately linked to household poverty, one male informant also described a joint decision made with his wife that, after losing his job, she should begin "self trading" for the survival of the family. According to him, women who "wait for the husband only to make the family survive is a problem," not only in the event of job loss, but also in cases where the primary breadwinner becomes disabled or dies. For his wife, previously "just a housewife at home" and "not educated," he felt it was important that she "be able to survive with the children" (Participant 68) on her own.

As a result of poverty and hardship at home, the majority of the women interviewed cited "work," "jobs" and "making money" as their main motives for migrating. However, for a few, seeking a "better life" went beyond the economic push factors described above, and included dissatisfaction with the political situation in their countries of origin.

A number of women from Zimbabwe cited politics, and more specifically "political corruption," as a major push factor. One male informant described a female friend's decision to migrate as follows:

> There are two reasons why she left the country ... one was for economic reasons.... The other reason was a political – what she tells me is ... that they are – they put political situation at her country, there it was so tense the other–, how can I call it, those who are in power are not accommodating of other views you see, so it's not safe as far as she's concerned, is not safe to stay there with the different views of things (Participant 62).

Several Mozambican migrants also cited political unrest and conflict as key factors in their decisions to travel to South Africa.

Finally, a number of participants described the treatment, and limitations on women's rights, in their countries as contributing factors in their decision to migrate. For example, one long-term migrant felt that while "a man is a man in Lesotho," in South Africa "women are taken care of" and "it's fifty-fifty" between the sexes (Participant 6). A male informant from Swaziland also commented that his wife, herself a Swazi national, came to South Africa seeking "a better life," including "birth" and "citizen rights." Gender roles in Swaziland specifically were also debated in one Johannesburg Focus Group, where women participants felt the country's king was "overdoing it" by continuing to take young wives, sometimes "by force, even if the child is not complete with school" (Focus Group 4, Participants 2 & 3). Finally, a Kenyan migrant participating in a Johannesburg Focus Group described both female genital mutilation, and the unequal treatment of women as major push factors in her decision to leave home:

> I lived in a village ... [in] Eastern Kenya. We were suffering there, and there was a group of men which circumcised ladies. Then I was doing Form 4 in school, they killed people and sliced them, so I said no, I can't stay here, I will go to my brother in South Africa. I didn't finish school because of that, so I wanted to come here and my father had to sell his farm so that I could come here.... [In Kenya], they broke our tribes up, they make you sell your possessions and women don't have a say in this, and the men go and spend their money with other women (Focus Group 2, Participant 4).

Beyond the largely economic, political and poverty-induced push factors that influenced MVP participants to leave their countries of origin, SAMP also sought to understand how expectations about destination countries affected migration decision-making. Although a few women said they had "no idea" of what to expect, most had preconceptions about their destination countries and set out seeking "greener pastures" or, one said, "egoli" (South African colloquial generally referring to Johannesburg as the "city of gold").

Many women felt South Africa could offer them a range of economic opportunities, as well as commodities and consumer goods unavailable at home. For some women, the prospect of "money" in itself was a major pull factor, often due to the appeal of stronger foreign currencies. Other women had simply heard that "in South Africa there is money" (Participant 21), and this in itself proved a strong pull factor. And with the prospect of "money" came a number of other economic desirables, including social assistance, access to basic necessities, and the ability to purchase particular commodities:

> Of course they said in South Africa it is better and the food is cheap and it is easy to find food (Participant 29).

> South Africa is a beautiful and rich country and it can think for the people because my kids are born here in South Africa. So they get child support grant and the government is better because old people get old age grant and other countries don't do that. And people living with AIDS get grant (Participant 16).

> I wanted to go and look for money. I first of all saw people from South Africa – they were having a lot of money and they were eating nice food, and clothes, and everything was looking so nice, that is why I decided to come to this country (Participant 34).

Most MVP participants, however, expected that they would be able to find work, or opportunities for business or trade in South Africa. Before leaving Zimbabwe, one described her positive expectations of South Africa, based on stories from other migrants:

> [In South Africa] you can find a job, work for yourself, manage to bring up your family, you can do everything that you want therefore to assist your family (Participant 26).

While the prospect of "many job opportunities" (Participant 5) in destination countries such as South Africa certainly differed from the realities experienced by many women, positive expectations and imagery constituted a significant pull for many.

Although many migrants had expectations of wealth, economic opportunity and a "better life" elsewhere, this was often coupled with fears about coming to South Africa. Based on stories from friends, family and other migrants, a number of women recounted stories they had heard describing South Africa as a dangerous and violent country where, according to the accounts heard by one Malawian woman, "there are police who arrest people a lot, people kill other people, [and] there is a lot of war" (Participant 9). Similarly, a migrant from Zimbabwe heard that South Africa was a "bad country, depending on crime" (Participant 19). A second Zimbabwean migrant heard even more terrifying stories of life in South Africa, although these were dispelled during her own personal experiences of travel:

> When people talk in their country, like you, you don't travel, some of you, when they go to Zimbabwe they have perceptions that the Zimbabweans eat human flesh, and of which that's not true. And the same thing used to be said at home about South Africans, so those rumours that are being spread all over (Participant 46).

In spite of such negative perceptions, push forces in countries of origin were still sufficiently strong to motivate women to migrate, in spite of potential risks.

Again in keeping with Dodson's findings, many of the women stated that members of their families, households and communities had responded negatively to their decision to migrate.[24] Women who met with resistance and discouragement recounted that this was generally due to perceived risks and dangers in destination countries:

> [My family] got different ideas, some they thought it was not good because South Africa is a dangerous place, something like that.... They don't have a choice, they have to let me do what I have to do at the end of the day (Participant 35).

> At first it wasn't easy for [my family] to accept [my decision to migrate] because they were worried that I might be killed in South Africa (Participant 46).

> Many of my family was discouraging me, they told me many things about South Africa. They said I could lose my belongings; I can get shot or what, so I was discouraged. The first time it was difficult for me, but at the end they supported me (Participant 43).

> [My family] didn't support me in any way because everyone was telling me negative things about the countries so that I can get discouraged, but there was nothing I can do. I wanted to migrate anyway. So I had to migrate (Participant 18).

One student from Botswana whose family was "not too happy" with her decision to move to South Africa attributed South Africa's image as a "violent" and "rough country" to the media, and stated that her parents still "check on me everyday" (Participant 1). These negative responses were not only true amongst the families of migrants traveling to South Africa: a South African woman who had returned from working in London recalled how it had been "tough" to convince her family "that I could make it on my own in another country" (Participant 54). Perhaps anticipating similar responses, five participants stated that they had simply left home without telling anyone where they were going.

Despite the negative responses and discouragement, MVP participants did make the decision to migrate. This is likely indicative of the strength of the mainly economic push factors many faced. But it is also perhaps indicative of agency in migration decision-making, in keeping with historical analyses that suggest "women have been practising independent migration across the borders of Southern African for decades."[25] Certainly for the women interviewed, discouragement from family did not translate into a deterrent to leave home.

Although less common, some women received support from their families and communities. This was the case when families felt there were no opportunities at home, as described by two long-term migrants from Zimbabwe:

> [My family was] very glad because in Zimbabwe it's useless to be there whilst you are not working (Participant 34).

> It's like they were willing that I can come here so that I can help my family with other things they can't afford to do (Participant 26).

A migrant from Malawi added that her family had responded positively to her short-term travel to South Africa when she began remitting money home. Other women reported that family responses were more positive when they were joining partners or other family members abroad, rather than traveling on their own to destination countries.

Overall, women devoted relatively little time during the interviews to discussing logistical arrangements, although the cost of travel was a concern to many. They did recount purchasing some goods for personal use and resale, and also seeking contact details for other migrants already living in destination countries through networks of family and community members. A clear difference did emerge between women who had travelled through "regular," or legal means across borders, and those who had traveled "irregularly." While regular migrants talked mostly about obtaining passports and visas, irregular migrants focused more on finding means to cross national borders without being detected.

OBTAINING TRAVEL DOCUMENTS

SAMP's earlier research indicated that in Southern Africa, women sampled had "a higher incidence of legal migration than male migrants."[26] Further 95% of women who had been to South Africa possessed valid passports at the time of their departure, compared to 86% of the men sampled.[27] Analysis of MVP texts generally confirmed that many women preferred to travel through regular and legal means. At the same time, many women felt the costs associated with regular travel were prohibitive, including visa fees and Customs duties. As a result, they had either chosen to cross borders irregularly, or to overstay their visas after arriving legally as visitors. Of the fifty migrants interviewed, sixteen explicitly stated that they had either entered South Africa illegally or had overstayed their visas.

Those who travelled through regular means found that obtaining travel documents was relatively straightforward. Visa applications were somewhat more complex for migrants entering destination countries for purposes other than a temporary visit, as in the case of a student from Botswana enrolled at a South African University:

> In terms of preparations, [I got] the permit that is required and also prepared accommodation when you get there, and a medical certificate.... The other thing, I had to have a passport, but I've always had a passport. I didn't need a visa … [but I needed] proof of residence and proof that you have enough funds … to cover your fees and to sustain yourself without having to rely on resources of the government. They need assurance that after completing your studies you will go back to your country. So I think it's R2000 is security for transport (Participant 1).

The most serious obstacle to obtaining a passport or visa was the cost of application fees, rather than problems in the application process itself. Although women from different countries discussed prohibitive costs associated with travel documentation, this was particularly problematic for Zimbabweans, whose nationals require visas to enter South Africa:

> It's difficult [to get a visa] because they give you too many papers and they ask you why you are going there, and that, do you have the money to spend there. If you don't have money they only register you to stay for one week. After one month they will see what they can do (Participant 12).

> It was difficult because South Africa wants a visa when you come from Zimbabwe. So to have a visa you need to have

money. So I couldn't because I didn't have money.... I think the last time it was R1000.... It is difficult because women can't follow it. So you find they risk their lives because they want to cross and come this side.... So I think it is difficult, at least if there were no visas it was going to be easy. Visa makes people suffer (Participant 28).

I can't say for other people's countries, but for my country [Zimbabwe] is difficult 'cause we're not given visas, you have to have a visa to come here. So if you don't have, you can't come.... It's not [easy to get a visa].... Is like they want money, it costs a lot to have a visa (Participant 50).

In spite of the high cost, many women took care to ensure that they had legal travel documents before migrating. At the same time, in the context of high levels of unemployment and household poverty, high visa costs ultimately pushed some to travel through irregular means, and others to overstay permitted time periods after entering their destination countries.

The women used a range of different modes of transport in migrating, often in combination. These included private cars, trains, airplanes, boats, trucks and traveling by foot, although most described traveling either by bus or by mini-bus taxi. A number of women felt that cross-border transport was too expensive, but nonetheless readily available:

It is not so difficult to get transport because there is usually transport every day coming here in South Africa. Like if you want to go to Johannesburg, there are buses and mini-buses going there, so you see that transport isn't difficult (Participant 2).

Arranging transportation for travel seemed to require minimal preparation and most modes were viewed as easily accessible, if costly. However, this was not the case for irregular migrants, who more often travelled by foot, truck or private car. In such cases, migrants described making contact with individuals known to assist in illegal border crossings. For this service, many paid high fees, traveled dangerous routes and risked discovery and arrest (see below).

Before leaving, women commonly purchased a range of goods. Long-term migrants were less likely to purchase goods or stock for resale. In fact, aside from personal belongings and food for their journey, several long-term migrants mentioned that they preferred to purchase goods such as new clothing when they arrived because they believed it would be cheaper:

No, I don't buy anything, I just slaughter a chicken for the journey. Things like clothes we buy here in South Africa (Participant 16).

I bought clothes, but mostly I buy here because when you look at the Rand/Pula exchange rate, when you convert Rands to Pulas, you get less money, so it's better to buy at this side (Participant 2).

Short-term migrants were much more likely to purchase goods in countries of origin for sale in South Africa, and in many cases were engaged in regular cross-border trade. They tended to buy goods they felt would be unavailable in South Africa, such as "African" clothing and sandals, handicrafts and curios, but also stock including conventional clothing and "safety boots," broomsticks, baskets, blankets, curtains, spinach, cloth, cosmetics, and garlic crushers. Several migrants from Zimbabwe also purchased decorative doilies and cotton for crocheting doilies, a craft that remains popular amongst market traders and is still used as "a way of earning a living if all else fails."[28]

Women seldom mentioned securing advance accommodation before leaving home, in either the in-depth interviews or the Focus Groups. Instead, they described sourcing other migrants already living in destination countries through family and community networks. For example, a migrant from Lesotho said that she had heard only about "someone whom I know to be a doctor" (Participant 4), and had set out for South Africa hoping this contact could give her a job and a place to live. A second migrant left Swaziland with only the address of an aunt who might be able to accommodate her (Participant 16). Similarly, a migrant from Mozambique knew only that her grandmother was in South Africa, but left home without even an address, hoping to find her after arriving (Participant 10). Migrants without any place to stay after arriving in South Africa sought out nationals from their own country for advice or information about accommodation and employment.

LEAVING HOME AND FAMILY BEHIND

Many of the women encountered their first real difficulties upon leaving home, and in particular, leaving behind their children, family members and friends. After the emotional difficulty of departing, however, women traveling through regular means with travel documentation experienced relatively few problems, beyond long waits in queues at border posts and poor service from officials in some cases. Traders also told of problems experienced in declaring goods at Customs, over-charging on Customs duties, and producing receipts and value-added tax (VAT) certificates.

Challenging the image of women as the "baggage of male workers," many migrated without partners or spouses and left family behind, including parents, siblings, and in many cases, one or more dependent children. Migrant women generally left their children in the care of their own parents or siblings, or with members of their extended family. One migrant from Zimbabwe stated:

> I left my children only. They stay by themselves, what can I do? My sister is taking care of them, she also gives them food. And when I get money here I sent it for them even though the money I get here is little, because when they buy mealie meal it is finished (Participant 23).

Less frequently, women chose to leave their children at home alone, feeling that income earned in South Africa and remitted to the family was most important. In one instance, a migrant described leaving her son at home alone in Lesotho; although her own mother was sometimes available to look after the child. Nonetheless, she felt her child would benefit most from the money she was able to send to him from South Africa:

> At home who is left is my mother, but … she's only there when there is trouble. The person left in the family is my son. I'm the one taking care of him, because when I'm at work, I send money for him. He's staying alone at home (Participant 4).

Leaving children and other family members behind in countries of origin was exceedingly difficult for many of the women interviewed. Separation from children proved emotional and distressing for many women migrants:

> Here I stay with my husband and my children are staying with my mom [in Malawi]. They are facing many problems, like when they are sick and when they need my love like their mother, but I can't do all those things because I am here because of them. So that I can get something for them for school, that is why I am here (Participant 40).

> It was difficult [to migrate], I wished to stay in my house…. I didn't like coming here because my children are not yet grown up, they are still small (Participant 23).

Others described the difficulty of leaving behind dependent and elderly parents, as well as close siblings and extended families. While several migrants said that partners, children, family members or friends had accompanied them to their transport departure point or to the border, many others left home alone.

TRAVELING THROUGH BORDER POSTS

Most of the women migrated through legal channels with the travel documentation required. Aside from some complaints about long queues, discomfort due to heat, and a lack of toilets and other facilities, most described their border crossing experiences as relatively easy. A number commented that they had not experienced any problems at the border, and that they had been treated "nicely" by Immigration officials. They were clearly aware of the difference a visa or passport made: "They did not treat me bad; they treat you bad when you don't have an ID and when you are crossing illegal" (Participant 45).

Women traveling on buses also mentioned that drivers often spoke to Immigration officials, paid required Customs duties, and were prepared to assist migrants with any difficulties encountered. A commercial bus driver highlighted some of the problems migrants encounter, stating that at one border post in particular the "boys working there sometimes come in drunk, they demand a bribe for you to pass," although he felt the "government does not know that such a thing is happening." This resulted in long queues of cars waiting to cross the border and "discomfort for passengers, since it will be very hot" (Participant 73).

Although most of the women traveling through legal border posts did not feel their experience was difficult overall, they did describe problems with transporting goods and paying Customs duties. Women who identified themselves as vendors or traders, in particular, felt that they were over-charged at the border, and one migrant from Zimbabwe described with regret how she had experienced a serious profit loss when she failed to declare her goods, and these were seized by officials (Participant 43). Other women opted to declare their goods rather than risk losing them, but this was sometimes costly and reduced profits from trade. In such cases migrants had become familiar with the processes of making Customs declarations and paying duties at the border:

> We don't have any problems except when we have to go pass Swaziland officials, it's then we have to pay if you bought stock of more than a thousand, but when it's less than that you don't pay, you just register the amount that you bought for, or the money exchange.... There are declaration forms that you fill then and sign in case when, where you bought crafts from Swaziland to South Africa, you would pay so as we when we go to Swaziland. I've never had a problem (Participant 42).

> I think it is expensive, like this, when you want to claim that

there is a, I think there is export duty. They fill the form, by filling that form you have to pay them. I think it's official. It does [affect my profit] because I declare being in Botswana border and I pay them in South African border. So far I haven't experienced anything that is bad (Participant 35).

Overall, women with travel documentation felt that the prospect of traveling in relative safety through legal border posts outweighed the difficulties and discomforts of irregular migration.

JUMPING THE FENCE

The experiences of women traveling through irregular means showed a stark contrast. After a difficult separation from family and friends, women who "jumped the fence" recounted traveling dangerous paths to avoid border posts, crossing rivers as well as forest and veld terrain, experiencing constant fear of being detected and caught, and falling victim to abuse by their transporters, as well as by security and border officials.

Many women who chose to travel through irregular means felt that the cost of a visa was prohibitive, or that the process of obtaining a passport was insurmountable. Rather than restricting the movement of women without real means to travel legally, visa regimes pushed them to seek irregular modes of travel, at major risk to their personal safety. One Zimbabwean migrant stated that her husband had died and, left as the sole breadwinner for five children, she decided to come to South Africa. After attempting to apply for a visa, she considered her options and decided on the cheaper alternative of paying R500 to be transported to the border at Beitbridge, where she crossed illegally into South Africa:

When you apply for a visa they ask you a lot of questions and it's expensive. I realized that it would be difficult for me to get it, and I talked to people who usually go to Johannesburg and they told me that I only need to have R500. They took me and left me at Beitbridge, and from there it was bad and it was difficult for me to pass through there…. I don't have traveling documents and I'm relying on these people and they left me there all alone by myself and they went through crossing the border. And when I was left there alone I met two ladies who joined me, and we slept there trying to find a way to get through to South Africa. We just slept on the fields around there and late at night we crossed the border because people were not many. We spent three days there wondering what we will do, I was thinking about my children back at home because I told my children that I was going to work at Johannesburg. After those three days we met truck drivers and we talked to them, they took us and dropped us off at Musina because that's where they were going, and we took off from there (Focus Group 3, Participant 5).

A sense of urgency and desperation, combined with the perception that legal travel documents were entirely inaccessible, prompted other migrants to travel through irregular means. In the case of a migrant from Swaziland, this meant crossing the border from South Africa with the dead body of her husband, whom she felt needed to be buried in Swaziland. Turned away at the border post because she only had a birth certificate for her baby, she instead chose to "jump the fence":

> As now I am South African and I have a South African ID and passport.... It was that time my husband passed away so I had my six-months old baby and I didn't make a passport for her. I only had a birth certificate so I had to ask to cross. They then said I had to go back because I don't have a passport for the baby. My five year-old has a passport, so I went back, then I crossed illegally because I had to go and bury my husband. I had to go back and jump the fence ... it was at night. It took us about thirty to forty minutes away from the border post. We had to cross reed, forest, and snakes would have eaten us, and they never cared that we had a dead body with us.... At that time it didn't matter, as long as I buried my husband (Participant 16).

Although women who chose to travel through irregular means often shared the common feeling that they had no other option, their migration experiences varied considerably. While some migrants travelled by foot across national borders, others arranged private cars to transport them into South Africa. In one case, the driver of the car negotiated entry into South Africa by bribing an Immigration official:

> I won't say they treated us badly because I didn't see harassment or anything like that, because whatever they want they talk to the driver and that is all. They don't talk to us because already I would have spoken to the driver that I don't have the passport and the papers. So when the driver arrives there he talks to them and I just sit only. They don't do anything to me. To me I can say it was easy. I did not come across any difficulties.... I did not come the legal way. I just came the illegal way. I did not get the passport. I just carried my ID for in case and my baby's things. I used a pri-

vate car. When I arrived at the border I just sat in the car and the person that I was with went in and produced his passport and also produced car papers and I just passed, and when I arrived at the gate, when they wanted my passport, he gave them money (Participant 28).

Participants from different countries in a Johannesburg Focus Group also discussed bribing Immigration officials at various border posts in order to gain entry, or to secure a permit for a longer period of stay:

We don't have a visa anymore [in Mozambique], but these people are bothersome even if there is no more visa. If we want to go there, they should give us 30 days. When you get there it depends on whether that person that's going to help you is happy on that day or not. You'll get to the border gates, they'll ask where you're going and you'll say Johannesburg. They'll tell you that they are giving you 3 days and if you ask for 30 days they'll refuse. They want you to hit the table. You should give them money, give them R50.00.... They'll ask what you're going to do there and if you say I'm just going to visit. They'll tell you that I'll give you five days. 'No, please I beg you.' You beg them with cash, you have to give them R50.00 or R20.00, it all depends, and you'll have to give them the money that they'll want for 30 days. But that 30 days is legal, they, they want the money, so that they can give you those 30 days. If you don't give them the money, they give you only 5 days to come here and go back, again.... They don't give you a receipt, it is their pocket money (Focus Group 4, Participant 3).

A second participant from the same Focus Group commented that this was true of Immigration officials in other SADC countries as well:

Even with us people from Malawi, people from Mozambique and Zimbabwe make us pay. We from Malawi. When we pass in Zimbabwe from Mozambique we pay R10.00. If you don't have R10.00 they'll send you back home to Malawi, so we pay the R10.00. When we get to the border gates, we also pay R50.00, at Nyamaphanda border post in Zimbabwe ... there are no receipts at all. It's the money for their own personal use. We bribe them (Focus Group 4, Participant 5).

A third participant added, however, that bribery was not necessary "all of the times" when crossing borders:

It's not all of them. Not all of the times does that happen;

there are those that have kind hearts and those that don't. Those that give us trouble are the ones that are not okay. They are just not kind, because they love money too much. Money they don't work hard for. They'll do funny things and be rude on you (Focus Group 4, Participant 1).

Women at a Focus Group in Makhado agreed that the prospect of bribing Immigration officials at the border was preferable to risking travel by foot around border posts:

Coming from home up to here, is not easy, we will be shivering. There is a code at the border post we call it diarrhea in our country; we call it a running stomach. You don't know what the officers they are going to say to you. The officer will say go back or come back and maybe you find that you find a piece job the officer will give you two days you see. Starting from the border is bad so for you to if you want to be clever they all agree with you, if your passport, if you don't want any problem put money inside the passport and give the Immigration officer then the Immigration officer will ask you how many days do you want. (Laughter). And when you say two months he'll say yes 'mam (Focus Group 6, Participant Unknown).

[Bribery] is working cause if you don't have money you'll get two days or you'll never get to enter South Africa at that border post, at that Beitbridge border post. ... this other ladies they can say hayi, we used a crocodile, they don't use the river. Even if your passport has expired you put money and you give an officer, you will get a pass to South Africa (Focus Group 6, Participant 5).

In these cases, migrant women appear to be crossing regional borders themselves and negotiating terms of entry and stay directly with Immigration officials; however, a more common experience involved traveling to the vicinity of a border and, after arriving, identifying persons in the area paid to assist in irregular crossings, referred to as *malaisha* (often applied to drivers, meaning "to carry") by Zimbabwean migrants. Women who "jumped the fence" by walking around established border posts, usually with a paid guide or *malaisha*, faced arduous journeys that included crossing rivers and difficult terrain, and the stress of constant fear and vulnerability to detection by Immigration officials, border security and police; attacks by wild animals; and even abuse and victimization by their paid guides. Irregular migrants from Malawi and Zimbabwe described their fears in crossing the border illegally into South Africa:

I didn't prepare anything, I just came with the *malaisha*, I just paid the money for *malaisha*. They carry cross borders. We pass by the forest.... You can get hurt, you can die there since they say there are wild animals, it might happen that I could die, and you go with the fear (Participant 31).

If you don't have the right documents you are going to go around in the bush. Then in the bush there are snakes.... I was with some guys waiting at Katembe and we saw people who are being eaten by crocodiles in the water. Sometimes you find a head, skeleton of a person who died a long time ago. And you find people who help people to get into South Africa – sometimes they rape you and take your money. Sometimes they shoot you if you don't want them to rape you (Participant 9).

There are taxis, which you have to hire, and at the border you have to jump because we are illegal. Under the fence there are boys who lives in the bush who help us to cross the border. When we reach Buckbridge Border we have to go to the bush at night, not during the day, at night, then we have to go under the fence or over the fence, then we have to look for the transport when we reach the Messina border. There are guys there who can take you and show you the way, and sometimes they can rape you or take all your belongings, they are very cruel because they don't listen to you when you are talking, they just want you to listen to all their instructions. When they want to rape you they can kill you. There are shortest ways and longest ways, some can take two hours, some you can take more than that (Participant 34).

While some women crossed the border with paid guides and were then left to their own devices, in other cases transporters contacted family members or acquaintances of the migrants in order to secure payment or arrange a drop-off. A Mozambican woman described how, after being guided across the border, her boyfriend was contacted by her transporters to arrange payment of a R400 fee, and to schedule a drop-off time at his home in Soweto:

I did not use transport, I just jumped the fence. From home we use cars and they place us next to border gate and wait for sunset. They are those people whom help us to jump the fence. They are next to the border gate, there are houses there … they used to helping people jump the fence, this people help us and take us to their homes and maybe by 8h00 or 9h00 pm we take our bags, or maybe we have children … this brothers help us climb the mountain and we walk from there. There are stones, grass and trees but we walk and until we reach a place where they know. They have houses in Maputo and they have houses in South Africa, so they place us in their houses, they ask us one by one who was going where … and they will ask whom are you staying with…. They would like to know the telephone number of this person, and they talk to him on the phone and they will ask if that person knows me and they will tell him that they are bringing me and then they will deliver us one by one. And we pay R400 each person for the fact that he helped me jump the fence (Participant 14).

Interview texts suggested that irregular migrant women experience sexual exploitation, abuse and rape all too frequently. Rape is one of the greatest fears in traveling through "the bush" and women are victimized by men paid to guide them into destination countries. A number described trading sex with Immigration officials or police in order to cross a border or avoid arrest. In the view of Focus Group participants from Johannesburg, irregular migrant women are regularly coerced into sex by South African Immigration and police officials:

The police will arrest you, but if you sleep with him they won't. I'll tell them I'm from Zimbabwe. If they see that you're beautiful, they then propose to you and you'll leave with them. If you sleep with them, they'll tell you go…. They check you as you approach. Even inside and taxis from across the border they take beautiful ladies and you'll meet up with them at the police station. When they would have had sex with the girls as a form of payment for being illegal. They would have finished with the beautiful ones…. You see, if a person wants to sleep with you they don't propose to you, they won't tell you that they love you, and you'll also not tell him that you love him. He will tell you to give him money, and if you don't have, he'll pull you to the side and the next thing he'll touch you. He tells you that if you don't have any money, let's do this and that. He'll tell you to sleep with him and do all those things, you see, even with you and I, I can see what is happening, like whatever happens at the border gates I can see, but the one thing that I see is that the police will sleep with the girl at the border gates. They'll even make a girl cross to Petersburg, so that they can have sex with her in their van (Focus Group 4, Participant 8).

A Makhado Focus Group participant described being met by "soldiers" who "demanded sex" while crossing through Beitbridge to enter South Africa:

> It was in 1993 my husband left me with two kids, he decided to go on with his program, so I decided to come to South Africa. I went to Beitbridge on foot up to the river. I didn't have any money, any passport, it was through the rural areas that I walked from there to the river and it was at night, at the river we found soldiers who wanted money if we did not have money they demanded sex. I slept with the soldiers because I didn't even have a single cent, then I crossed to the farms next to the Limpopo to work there (Participant 5, Focus Group 5).

A Mozambican migrant in the Johannesburg Focus Group described witnessing police officers on a train having sex with a young woman whom she believed to be an irregular migrant. Witnessing this encounter had, in itself, proved extremely traumatic:

> I saw something very painful on my way home.... You know sad things happen in the train. When I think about it – I don't know – at the time there were police from the border gates entering. They were trying to stop the people that sell alcohol from coming inside because those people sell alcohol and send, they steal people's belongings.... I saw something painful. I saw something very painful, there was this white policeman that saw a young girl, you see? These black officers were on the lookout for other people on behalf of this man. He was having sex with this girl. You see there at the doors? These guys were on the lookout so that there won't be anyone coming in since it is the last coach. This police was having sex with this girl.... If you don't have an I.D. right? This person is younger than I am and you're the police officer. You're here to search people in the train; you'll stop searching people to go see the other one you'll take her to the door.... Because I don't have an I.D. and no passport, you'll have to have sex with him. What else can you do? (Focus Group 4, Participant 1).

Other migrants in this Focus Group conceded that even if "We don't agree with our heart," women submit to forced and coercive sexual acts "because it's compulsory."

Stories told by MVP participants highlighted the extreme vulnerability of women migrants, especially those who travel through irregular means, as well as the gravity of the abuse and exploitation they face. These experiences also point to the real need for added measures to promote and protect the rights of female migrants, and to put an end to exploitation and corruption amongst Immigration and police officers. Furthermore, promoting access to immigration-related information and making visas and travel documents more affordable and accessible would have a real impact in encouraging migrant women to travel through safe and regular channels across borders.

MIGRATION AND PERSONAL CHANGE

Most of the women interviewed for the MVP were motivated to leave home for economic reasons, citing work, trade, shopping and a better life as the main reasons for migrating. Many also had high expectations about the economic opportunities available to them in destination countries. As shown, the quality of women's travel experiences differs dramatically between those who travel through regular, legal channels and those who "jump the fence" and are often victims of abuse and exploitation. In spite of these enormous differences, most women agreed that they underwent major changes upon arriving in their destination countries, personally, in terms of their individual economic status and the circumstances of their households and families. In most cases, women felt that the quality of their lives had improved, and therefore that the impacts of migration were mainly positive.

Many of the participants felt that they had undergone major personal change since arriving in South Africa. One migrant from Swaziland described her personal learning and growth while living in South Africa as follows:

> You just kind of glow and life is brilliant, and I just understand a little more about life. I think it's in every situation that you put in, there's always so much to learn. I can't say it's specifically because I came to South Africa, and even if I could go to America to work I would still get the same thing (Participant 17).

A second migrant from Zimbabwe had initially been concerned about being "with people from different cultures in different countries," but had become accustomed to this through her frequent travels:

> The only thing is that when it's your first time here and you are not used to interact with people from different cultures in different countries you'll be worried because you don't

33

know them, but now I'm used to all of this because I'm used to traveling (Participant 46).

However, for many women, positive personal change was also related to individual identity. Women felt they had more choice in terms of the clothing they were able to purchase and wear in another country, use of different languages, and access to different consumer goods:

> I think South Africa opened my mind in terms of fashion. It has a variety of different people and culture … and when it comes to the language, they use a lot of slang (Participant 1).

> Here in South Africa I speak Zulu. I learned through speaking to other people. Life has really changed for me here in South Africa 'cause I have met different people from different countries, I mean it has changed. Living a life, okay now I can say I am living a different life because I mean things here are cheaper. Things like the home theatre system, I mean, household things like microwave, and the clothing too (Participant 18).

For a woman from Mozambique, real lifestyle improvements had come from access to a broader range of rights, although as a non-citizen she felt that these were not always applicable to her own circumstances:

> It has changed a lot because the rights here in South Africa are better than those in Mozambique. Well, they say a person has a right to work, but for me it's difficult because I'm not a South African. And if you are educated there is a big chance that you will make it in a big way. So there in Mozambique even if you are educated it's difficult to find a job. Only a few people have money to further their studies and work (Participant 10).

Interestingly, while migrant women embraced some personal changes that they felt strengthened their own sense of identity and freedom, many also struggled to preserve particular elements of their own culture or upbringing. This proved difficult for some. While one migrant felt that her life was "better" after leaving Lesotho, she was concerned that people in South Africa had "lost their culture":

> South Africa's lifestyle is fast, it's too fast and most people have lost their culture, but from where I come from, culture is much valued, there's respect, honour, etc. It's better [in South Africa] but it's fast, it's so fast in a way that everything is happening so fast (Participant 5).

MIGRATION AND ECONOMIC CHANGE

MVP participants also felt that they had undergone major economic and financial changes since migrating. At the same time, while personal economic circumstances had dramatically improved, women acknowledged this was not without hard work. In the words of a Mozambican migrant, "I haven't experienced anything except that you have to work hard – if you don't work hard, what would you do, because everything is going to be difficult (Participant 13).

The general consensus amongst participants was that their economic circumstances, and therefore their overall quality of life, had improved after migrating. This is consistent with Dodson's earlier finding that both male and female migrants in Southern Africa felt migration had a "positive" impact on their lives.[29] Women stated that they could increasingly buy goods such as bread, cooking oil, rice, soap and clothing. The strength of South Africa's currency, as well as the range and availability of goods, also impacted positively on their ability to buy basic necessities:

> The only problem is of not finding a job, but the food is better because I can afford to buy…. I won't say I have money like that, but the conditions are better here than back home because I do get food and clothing and I am able to buy them (Participant 29).

> Nothing has changed except that when I am here I am able to make money. And the money that I'm making is able to make me live. It's not like Zimbabwe, like when my husband was getting paid month-end – after three days, I don't see the money any more. So when I am in Johannesburg it's better because things here are cheap, even though the money is little we try to live (Participant 28).

> It's not the same, as I was at home doing nothing. It's not the same since I'm here. Here I know I can get the bread and send money home (Participant 32).

> I love South Africa, because in this place we don't get into politics. We still get food, apples, bananas and biscuits with good money. If you have R20 then you know that you can buy food along with apples and cool-drinks with that R20 (Focus Group 4, Participant 1).

Economic improvement resulting from migration varied, with some women benefiting more than others through new jobs and business opportunities. Those who were able to earn more discussed consumer goods and commodities that they had never previously been able to afford, including new clothing, appliances, and electronic equipment such as CD and DVD players. With a higher income and greater access to commodities often came a newfound sense of independence.

A small group of participants had achieved substantial economic improvements and were able to invest their income, through purchasing businesses and houses. Again, this contributed to a sense of independence amongst the women interviewed. Chari suggests that economic activities emerging from migration, and cross-border trade in particular, have "transformed many unemployed women into breadwinners" and "given them some element of economic independence that is spilling over to other areas of their lives, e.g. social status, position in the household, [and] decision-making authority."[30] This was certainly true of the MVP respondents. A migrant from Malawi who was able to buy a house from the profits of her cross-border trade activities stated that, as a result of migrating, she had "everything that I needed," and added that "I am right now." Investments made by migrants also turned into income and wealth-generating activities; as a woman from Lesotho stated, "Now I'm able to do everything that I want. I do have furniture and four cars. I built [a house]. It's three rooms" (Participant 6).

While most of the women seemed to have benefited economically from migration, a small number felt their personal financial situation had actually worsened after leaving home. A migrant from Lesotho stated during an in-depth interview that her life "hasn't changed, in fact it's more difficult than before" (Participant 4). A second migrant from Mozambique had the same perspective. Although she was unsure of "how things would be now at home if I would be there," she still struggled to buy food and pay her rent.

HOUSEHOLD LIFESTYLE CHANGES

Beyond individual improvements, the benefits of new economic activities after migrating also significantly impacted on women's households and families. As has been found in other studies,[31] women migrants invested income from employment and trade primarily into providing for the needs of children, families and extended households. Women who felt better able to provide for the needs of their children, in particular, as well as other dependants such as elderly parents, expressed a sense of relief and newfound security. Remittances are a central part of this experience. One Zimbabwean woman found that, after migrating, "if my children need something I am able to do it for them one by one every month" (Participant 23). A second Zimbabwean migrant stated, "I send money every month – at least they are buying something" (Participant 25). Others commented:

> [My family's lifestyle] has changed because I find temp jobs so that I can send some money to my kids so they could eat (Participant 15).

> My mother [is in Swaziland] because my father passed away, and my brothers are there. When I get paid I make sure that I post them money – R100 or R200. The money is enough because at home we don't buy mealie-meal, we plough, so that money is for the meat. They even planted cabbage and spinach (Participant 16).

> Now I send money at home, and the business is better because I send money, sometimes I buy something like Vaseline and send it to home. Vaseline, soup, and send it to home (Participant 30).

> I can say my lifestyle changed – it has gone better, a little bit better. I am able to have my own money and I am able to support my own kids. I am able to go back to Zimbabwe and come back.... I can send [my family] everything they need, all kinds of groceries that I buy in South Africa, I send them to Zimbabwe (Participant 34).

> My mother is no longer worried because all of us, when we get money we help her. She is not worried about us because there are no young ones, instead we are the ones who are taking care of her when she needs something (Participant 13).

While many women aimed, first, to provide basic needs and food for families at home, their second priority was to invest in their children's education. A migrant from Malawi stated that "now I can afford to pay school fees and to take care of my children and the other family members" (Participant 39) and, similarly, a Focus Group participant commented, "I can buy things for my children and I can even pay for their school fees."

Women migrants not only prioritize investing in the education of their own children, but also that of their younger siblings left behind. For some, remittances meant that children who had not been attending school at all could begin to do so:

> Here things are cheap, at home it is not easy to get cheap things like this.... I see I changed a lot, because I know how

to support my mother and my younger sisters and brothers. They can go to school now because I send the money there, you see (Participant 30).

It has really changed. Since I've started the business I am able to assist my brothers and sisters. Like paying their school fees and food (Participant 42).

I can say there are a lot of changes in my family ... economically and financially. 'Cause most of my family – especially most of my sisters and brothers, they have changed schools and the household, we have better things like theatre systems. Everything is okay because I don't buy grocery that side, I bring it with me because this side, it is cheaper than that side (Participant 43).

Although a minority amongst the women interviewed, several migrants stated that they were "unemployed" and cited no other economic activities. One woman from Zimbabwe commented that her family's lives "haven't changed, they are just the same like before because I am not working and I am not able to buy them food or support them with anything" (Participant 29). The inability to contribute to household costs, and the welfare of family members left behind, remained a grave concern for some migrants:

I have got eight kids and four grandkids. I can't carry them all into South Africa. I can only bring two or three at a time. I have got a burden behind me, I have to take care of these children. Because of the border jumping I can't take all of them so if I can take three I can afford it, it's nice in South Africa, but when I sleep I think of the ones that I left at home, even if I can have a nice meal but when I think about the ones at home I can't eat it, something has to done (Focus Group 5 Participant 2).

NEW COUNTRY, NEW LIFE

Women's conclusions that their lives were "better" after migrating seemed to be contradicted by their social experiences. Migrants in South Africa face multiple forms of discrimination as non-citizens, as members of particular ethnic groups, as black Africans, as women, and because they were poor. Cumulatively, much of the discrimination experienced by participants was rooted in xenophobic responses from citizens of countries of origin.

As one said, there are "many problems, many negative experiences, and many scenes of discrimination that migrants and refugees face on a daily basis" (Participant 70). This is consistent with research conducted by SAMP in partnership with the South African Human Rights Commission (SAHRC), which found that "South Africans as a whole are not tolerant of outsiders living in the country" and showed "strong support for policies that would place strict limits on or prohibit immigration altogether."[32]

Despite the resolve expressed by Minister of Home Affairs Nosiviwe Mapisa-Nqakula in 2004 to implement an immigration policy that reflects both South Africa's "commitment to human rights" and "commitment not to discriminate on the basis of gender," the experiences of MVP migrants suggest that levels of xenophobia remain high.[33] Many participants recounted derogatory name-calling, harassment and abuse by citizens, police, and government officials, and were regularly restricted access to basic services such as health care and education. While some migrants found that amongst South Africans, "some are nice and some are bad," they were certainly aware of xenophobia directed towards migrants in general. Women who felt they had not experienced xenophobia and were treated "well" overall by citizens generally shared a language or ethnic group with South Africans, and therefore were able to integrate more easily.

IMPOSSIBLE INTEGRATION: TREATMENT BY CITIZENS

Many of the migrant women felt that they faced little or no prospect of social integration in the country, and were regular victims of harassment, abuse and exclusion by citizens. Perhaps the most common example of this was in near-relentless name-calling:

> People here treat us bad. They call us names like makwerek-were and everything (Participant 24).

> Even in the community you can see that you are treated differently. They call you names. Kwangkwang. It means a foreigner (Participant 18).

> These ones, they are worst to be honest with you, South Africans, they don't really like foreigners and they all us by names such as kwerekwere, which we don't like that (Participant 25).

> The treatment is not the same like other South African citizens. When I walk out in the street I look out for police

cars. If I can see it when I get back, they just see you walking and they will say to you, 'hey you, khalanga, come this
side!'" So. I don't know how they see you, but the truth is
that they do see you, that you are a khalanga and you are
from Zimbabwe (Participant 28).

You can say there is that harassment by officials because
today we've got names, it's not nice, those makwerekwere's,
it's not a nice word, it's an insulting word. So, when they use
those words to us it means they don't like us (Focus Group 5
Participant 2).

This regular name-calling and verbal abuse was a source of hurt and
humiliation for many of the migrants interviewed, and reinforced feelings of deep social exclusion. Migrants also described feelings of shock
and surprise at being met with such open hostility in South Africa. One
migrant from Zimbabwe had concluded that nationals of her own country
and of South Africa are "different people … even mentally," because of
the negative attitudes towards foreigners that she had encountered:

We are different people. Even when they know, we are not
the same, even mentally we are not the same…. They talk
things that are not appropriate to be said to people. That
people from outside must be arrested and should be brought
back to their country because they make South African citizen to be unemployed. Even the government saw that people from Zimbabwe are all over (Participant 32).

In explanation, a migrant from Lesotho who felt that South Africans
"treat you like dogs," felt this was because of the view that "we are the
Sotho and then we have no right to be here" (Participant 4).

Alongside the emotional and psychological effects of name-calling and non-acceptance, migrant women found it extremely difficult to
accept the negative stereotypes that South Africans held about non-
citizens. Past SAMP research has pointed to the role of the media in
the continued perpetration of negative stereotypes of migrants, who are
frequently depicted as "job stealers," "criminals" and "illegals."[34] One
long-term migrant explained that, upon first introduction South Africans
"welcome and treat us kindly." But subsequently "when they hear we are
from Zimbabwe their attitudes change" (Participant 33). A student from
Botswana observed:

I think that racism is the major thing that–, and I'm not
used to that. Like in restaurants, there were incidents where
I will arrive first and be served last. Even in varsity there
are certain things like making criteria, you'll find that my

problem was better than hers but – I think in the case of
xenophobia, I think it's just the case of ignorance because
other people would assume that you are from here, but the
minute you tell them that you're not from South Africa, it's
like – …. There were instances where you mentioned that
you are from another country and [they] perceive you as a
poor person using their resources (Participant 1).

This stereotype was one of many that migrant women encountered.
Others included perceptions that all foreigners are "desperate and poor,"
thieves and criminals, responsible for taking jobs from nationals, and that
women specifically, were "stealing" South African husbands. The tendency to blame foreigners for crime, as well as for taking South African jobs
and husbands, was a point of discussion amongst participants at a Focus
Group in Makhado:

Like where we stay, they said they want to remove us
they want to go house-to-house looking, and if there's a
Zimbabwean they must deport because they don't want foreigners in…. Some say that we women take their husbands
and we also take jobs … but it's not true. If they don't take
care of their husbands, what must we do? (Focus Group 5,
Participant 3).

I'm still on that issue of the problems we face, they say "the
Zimbabwean steal our things, they break our property at
night, they take bribes." Right they are going to deport us.
Before we came here in South Africa were there no robbers
and thieves, here in South Africa, were there no thieves
before Zimbabweans came? Now, when those people are
arrested, you hear them some are Vendas and Shangan
people and other are from these other ethnic group in
South Africa … but at the end of the day they'll say it's
the Zimbabweans who steal. What about thieves in South
Africa, where are they? (Focus Group 5, Participant 2).

In addition to being blamed for a range of problems in South Africa,
Focus Group participants felt negative stereotypes and xenophobia
excluded them from community events and organizations, such as meetings, associations and churches. After seeing a notice for a community
meeting while riding the bus, one woman explained how, when she had
been interested in attending, "they'll always talk about the Zimbabweans,
so we decided not to go there because when we go there they say these
Zimbabweans have come here to take our work, we will chase them
from South Africa." She had then attempted to convene her own "soci-
ety meeting," but had been told by community members, "if you are a

41

Zimbabwean you couldn't do your meetings unless you go to the civic," and "if you hold that meeting we'll call the police, and they'll come to arrest you" (Focus Group 5, Participant 3).

The difficulties of encountering xenophobic attitudes and negative stereotypes are compounded by a sense of injustice specifically related to how they felt foreigners were treated in their own countries of origin. The women tended to view their own countries as more hospitable to foreigners such as tourists and holidaymakers, including South Africans:

> There are different [people] from different countries that come for different reasons, but they are not chased away by my country, our president let them stay. But when we come here they chase us. We just ask ourselves, what did we do? Why does our president let people stay there? In Maputo there are so many tourists and they are being treated the same way as us. People of South Africa, sometimes they treat us just like dogs. They call us by names like makwerekwere, amazizimbane, they call us everything (Participant 14).

> [Citizens] are the problem, they call us kwerekwere – even in other countries there are people who travel there. Even in Malawi there are people from South Africa and we don't call them names because they are just like us. And those people, they don't come from overseas, they are from here. Here in Africa we are one, we don't cause them problems, we treat them as though they are our people (Participant 40).

MVP participants were puzzled by the treatment they encountered, as they had imagined that South Africans, particularly black South Africans, would be more welcoming:

> You find that other people here, they say here is a kwerek-were, but when they come to our country we don't say that [about] them. The boers, they come to take our fish and our houses but we don't say to them they are kwerekweres. We treat them as blacks because we are all blacks and we are the same, but people from here are sometimes rude. I had that problem but there are people talking around, like one day there were two girls talking to my friend saying you are a kwerekwere and you don't know our language, you come from far away.... I won't beat up this person because I know that we are all blacks and I don't know why they treat us like that. They don't know where I come from and how was my life and what kind of person am I.... Like me, I am braiding people's hair but some of them they like saying

things about me when they are with their friends, saying this kwerekwere, this and that, but I won't stop braiding them because I want money. I came here to work (Participant 9).

Without the prospects of social integration, migrant women often developed coping mechanisms and survival strategies for living in South Africa. Assimilation proved easiest for women from countries sharing common languages, cultures and ethnic groups with South Africa, such as Botswana, Lesotho and Swaziland. Several women from these countries felt that by assimilating they were accepted by nationals:

> They treat me well, they understand my language and my culture, and I also understand the thing that they do and their reasons for doing that, so we understand each other (Participant 2).

> [South Africans] are ok – I think that they like people from Swaziland. As far as I'm concerned, they are ok, I haven't had any bad treatment and I don't care, I just consider everyone to be equal (Participant 15).

> People here are very good and everybody in this area has treated me with respect, even the neighbours are good to me.... They don't treat us bad, they even want to learn our language, especially us from Swaziland (Participant 16).

Other migrants who are more visibly "foreign" do not receive the same treatment from citizens:

> In my view, they treat us fine compared to people from Mozambique and the northern part of Africa, because I speak seSotho and I can easily speak isiZulu, but those who are from Mozambique and etc. are easily identified from their accent that they are foreigners, so I don't have a problem that I'm also a foreigner (Participant 5).

> I've seen them treat those people who are darker in skin – I've seen them, South Africans. I've seen them treat people badly like in a taxi, I do speak a little Zulu, like in a taxi there is a lady next to me and she can't speak Zulu and the taxi driver will have an issue with that. Like if she speaks in English the driver will say in Zulu, 'I do not understand' (Focus Group 1 Participant 1).

Focus Group participants discussed changing their traditional styles of dress after arriving in South Africa, both as a strategy for assimilation and to avoid attention, particularly from the police. One migrant explained

that the police "know how we walk and how we dress: South Africans
put on trousers and Zimbabweans put on dresses." Another added
that she had asked her brothers to teach her how to "walk" like South
Africans before migrating in order to better assimilate (Focus Group 5).
Finally, women simply attempted to go about their daily lives unnoticed
wherever possible, and a Mozambican migrant commented that if "you
behave well you can be able to survive and never see the difference, you
will be the same like other people as long as you behave" (Participant
13).

Another strategy used by women is to live and work in communities
already populated by other migrants, including areas of downtown and
central Johannesburg such as Hillbrow:

> In Hillbrow we are all khalangas so we treat each other
> equally (Participant 28).

> I can't say its bad, the treatment is not bad as such there are
> some who hate foreigners and there are some who feel pity
> for foreigners. Like the community is all right because like
> here in Park Station they know that we are foreigners – they
> accept our problems (Participant 34).

Women felt that residents of these communities, including other foreigners, were more likely to be accepting. Others did accept that not all
South Africans were xenophobic:

> I can't say you see we are different. Your face is different
> to mine. That's how people are, some are good, some not,
> some treat us bad. You see we are not the same, some drink
> too many, especially young boys. Some help you if you say
> you were chased by someone with a knife, they help you. So
> I can't say 100%, maybe 90 out of 100, 10 percent are bad
> (Participant 49).

Some women felt that, as foreigners, they were not actually entitled to
treatment on a par with South Africans:

> When you are a foreigner, you are that, and you can't be
> treated the same as citizens (Participant 46).

> I can't demand that, I can't demand to be treated like a
> South African citizen and I'm not looking forward to being
> treated as one. I think [South Africans] are okay anyway,
> although there are a few that always calling people names
> like 'Hey, makhalanga' and things like that, even though
> I'm not a khalanga, so it's boring. It's like a person calling

you a Zulu and you know that you are a Xhosa. It's boring (Participant 19).

Others sought to mitigate the effect of xenophobia, for example, stating that that "doesn't bother me that much because it is not that bad" (Participant 29).

In contrast, returned South African migrants who had travelled in the region felt they were treated with warmth and hospitality in neighbouring countries:

> They did not treat me like a foreigner, they treated me like I was born in Swaziland (Participant 52).

> They were happy for me, everything was fine and I got many friends. They wanted to know more about South Africa, stuff like that (Participant 55).

> There was never a problem. They treated me like a princess, so they always wanted to be around me at all times. So it's like I was somebody special to them. It was like a privilege for them to have me around (Participant 57).

TREATMENT BY OFFICIALS AND POLICE

Beyond their day-to-day interactions with citizens, migrant women described their encounters with xenophobia from "the government" in South Africa, most often through interactions with police, Customs officials, and staff at public hospitals and clinics. While acknowledging that "the government" afforded them particular amenities they were unable to access at home, such as better schools, health services, and even a broader range of rights, women were nonetheless victims of verbal abuse and name-calling, discrimination, exclusion and, from police officers in particular, solicitation of bribes and sex.

While women did not necessarily feel entitled to the same rights and treatment by the government as South African citizens, they nonetheless expressed surprise, hurt, and indignation when met with xenophobic attitudes from government officials, and in public services and institutions. Government officials were said to have often used derogatory and xenophobic names when addressing migrant women. A Malawian woman stated that migrants were often referred to as grigambus by government officials and was particularly shocked by this, given that she felt nonnationals and traders in South Africa had created employment for citizens.

Migrant women interviewed suggested that they frequently encountered police officers who, as described by a Key Informant, "do not even know the Immigration Act, or immigration laws generally" (Participant 71). Beyond fear of arrest and deportation, which are legal strategies for migration control administered and enforced by government,[35] migrant women faced three main illicit and unlawful threats from police officers: extortion and solicitation of bribes; destruction of travel documents; and general exclusion from legal assistance, protection and basic services.

Extortion, and the solicitation of bribes, was a regular feature of interactions between migrant women and police officers. Women recounted that they were often "chased" by the police and threatened with arrest and deportation; rather than following through with legal procedures, police officers were described as demanding money, food or drinks, or goods and stock from traders. Rather than risk arrest, women would agree to the demands of police officers.

A commercial bus driver who frequently transports migrant women across borders stated that the "police are corrupt" and that "they treat these people very bad." He added that police officers "will always demand a passport" from foreign women. Where "a visa is left with one day to expire, they would say you are not supposed to be here, and then they would take something from that woman" (Participant 73).

Extortion and bribery were not only common at border posts, but in day-to-day exchanges between migrants and police officers. Three women from Mozambique and Zimbabwe, now living in Johannesburg, described demands made by police officers for "cold drinks" and money:

> It is not alright because police chase us all the time, they take our money, they say please buy me a cold drink. They know if I advertise myself as a hairdresser, and maybe the police arrive and ask for ID and passport and I would say, I don't have, they will say that, 'get in the car!' I will refuse and will tell them I have a child. And then they will say I am lying and they force me into the car and go around [the] location with me, and when they stop they will want a cold drink from me. We thought they want only R6 for cold drink, but will want R100 each person. Police makes our lives so difficult 'cause they want nothing else, they only want the money (Participant 14).

> We lived by hiding, even if I was selling, if I saw the police coming, I would leave the stock there and go inside the flat, you see? You just leave it there; there are those who sell next to you. They are from here in South Africa and had IDs; I left the stock with them. They say: 'Here comes the police',

I would get away from here to hide, because if they catch me I would have to give them money that I wouldn't receive as my wage. At the end of the week I'd get nothing, because that money I gave to the police (Focus Group 4, Participant 3).

[Bribing] is not nice because even now we do it; if you don't have money you'll be arrested and if you have it you survive through bribe. You see that these police, when they are sent to catch criminals, they don't do that instead they arrest us. They don't arrest criminals, but they are busy walking down the streets looking for IDs and passports. I wish that they should treat us fine and wherever we go they don't bother us. They should stop forcing us to bribe them. When they make us pay, money does not go to the Government but to their pockets. Now they don't want R50 anymore, but now if you give them R100 they tell you to go to hell, the money is just peanuts ... if you have money you are fine because you know that if you can be caught you'll bribe them (Focus Group 3, Participant 7).

A second major threat from police officers is the destruction of passports and identity documents. Women are aware that migrants sometimes carry fraudulent South African IDs. One Focus Group participant explained that "you take other peoples IDs and you just change the photos. If they put a fingerprint to the ID even a Zimbabwean can take that ID the fingerprint won't be the same" (Focus Group 2, Participant 6). However, the approach of police officers is to "tear first and talk later," irrespective of whether passports and IDs were valid or not. The destruction of documentation is often used alongside other intimidatory tactics:

[South Africans] call us by names, kwere-kwere and all other names, even the police call us by names and say if your government cooperate with ours then things could be better and they say we are going to arrest you because you are kwere-kwere – I even don't respond to them any more. When they arrest me, I show them my papers, if they tear them apart – in most case they use South African IDs they just change the photos that is why they tear them (Focus Group 2, Participant 5).

Women migrants often leave their passports and IDs hidden at home and risk arrest by police officers, as this is considered preferable to having documents destroyed altogether. A Mozambican migrant whose passport was torn up by police officers who "demanded money" said she has begun living "by ukubhanxa" (meaning a game of hide and seek with police).

Widespread suspicion and distrust of police officers is a natural consequence of ongoing intimidation and harassment. Many of the migrant women stated that they avoided the police altogether. One Focus Group participant from Uganda noted:

> Foreigners can't report crime because they are afraid (Focus Group 2, Participant 1).

Other women concurred:

> I wanted to open a charge. Then I said whatever I wanted to say this police guy said where is your passport. I said didn't come here for passport, attend my case then after that you can ask for my passport and arrest me after you have attended my case. I said might I see the commissioner – if you don't have a passport they'll just arrest you and deport you they would not help you, I don't know why.

> I mean like if you don't have the right documents and you are raped it's not the police problem but the person is scared to go there and report, you know, people are just scared if you are in a foreign country, it is natural you are not used to that place or to the people. They will say I'll end up being arrested (Focus Group 6).

Women migrants have come to expect harassment and abuse in everyday exchanges with police officers patrolling the streets, but they were particularly fearful of being taken into police stations and questioned or detained. Described by one woman as "apartheid in the police station" (Focus Group 4 Participant 8), foreign accents, dialects, and the inability of migrants to speak in local languages were viewed as triggers for poor treatment from police officers. A second woman stated that as soon as migrants began speaking in English, police officers and other officials would "know that you are not from here and they will start speaking their language and they will even insult you and then say go back to your countries, we don't need you (Focus Group 4, Participant 2). Women felt that they could never report a conflict or problem with a South African, as police officers always side with South Africans.

Migrant women who are brought to police stations often resort to bribery to avoid remaining in police custody. A Zimbabwean woman described how migrants generally paid bribes to police officers outside of stations to avoid being seen:

> The cops arrest us and the citizens and the community, they call us names. Like kwerekwere. Sometimes the cops,

they take you to the police stations and they make you pay
some money which makes it difficult because sometimes
you don't have the money…. That money would be a bribe
for policeman not to take you or make you stay in the cell
for a night…. We are afraid of staying in the cell so we do
the payment out of the police station, or maybe somewhere
outside of the police station, because if they take you to the
police station they will deport you or what. They want R300
per person (Participant 43).

This account is consistent with footage aired on the South African
Broadcasting Corporation's (SABC) investigative feature Special
Assignment in September of 2005. Public attention was drawn to police
officers from Booysen's station in Johannesburg "roaming the suburbs to
arrest immigrants" who were detained in "room 6A" until friends and
family members paid bribes for their release.[36]

Many of the women pay bribes to avoid being taken to the notorious
Lindela Repatriation Centre outside Krugersdorp in Gauteng. According
to Dr. Loren Landau, migrants who have "money" and "connections" are
"not likely to end up in Lindela."[37] However, migrant women who are
sent to Lindela are more distressed by the potential abuse they face at
Lindela than the prospect of being deported.

Fears about being detained at Lindela are not unfounded. A report
released by the Ministerial Committee of Enquiry (October 2005)
reported that 27 detainees died at Lindela between January and August
of 2005. The Committee found that "sleeping quarters are overcrowded
(some 50 inmates per room)," the "bedding and food supply is not opti-
mal" and there is "a communication problem in particular language barriers."[38] Citing reports by the South African Human Rights Commission,
Lawyers for Human Rights and other organizations, the committee:
"highlighted the poor conditions of detention at Lindela and confirmed
complaints of inhumane treatment and indignity of persons held at the
facility. The majority of complaints concentrated on the unlawful long
detention periods, inadequate nutrition, irregular or inadequate medical
care, general poor living conditions, limited access to information, assault
and the mistreatment of minors."[39]

Women who were without "money" or "connections," sometimes
resorted to trading sex with police officers to avoid being sent to Lindela.
A Focus Group participant in Johannesburg noted:

Sometimes they can use you. They can have sex with you.
Like when you come back he will tell you what he wants like
sex and most women fall for it, most women when they want
something they use sex, like when they are arrested they

> sleep with cops just to let them go, if the police men ask you for sex you must know that you are in trouble. [Police ask] all the time. They start by proposing you, asking for phone numbers. The police are working for the government and they are everywhere so they can ask you question then ask you for that something. Let's say that you are arrested and you don't have any money and he proposes, you will say yes just to get out, if they say that tomorrow you are going to Lindela you will do it just not to go home. They don't [offer to] do it, the police ask for it, they say if you need any help have sex with me. They rather sleep with a police than going to Lindela (Focus Group 2).

During the interviews and Focus Groups, a number of women shared their own experiences of being arrested and detained at Lindela. These stories revealed neglect, abuse and poor treatment, and solicitation of both monetary bribes and sex in exchange for being released from the facility. A Malawian migrant described how she had been arrested by police officers who refused to accept her bribes and took her to Lindela, along with three other migrants:

> I had a job in town and they found me on the street, and it was I and another sister and another girl and a boy from Zimbabwe. This boy from Zimbabwe had an ID, I and the sister and the girl, they took us to Lindela. When we tried to give them money they said they don't take money at the police station. When we were in Lindela we found some guys who take money – if you have R400 they let you go, if you don't have R400 you stay inside. The sister that we were with got out because she had the R400, but us, we didn't have the money – we went inside (Participant 9).

The same migrant said that she had witnessed officials "sharing" another detainee, and she herself had been propositioned in exchange for being released:

> The food was terrible and they didn't treat us well.... People of South Africa, they go to our country Malawi to visit but we don't do the things that they do to us. Girls here they have secrets – they share amongst themselves, and I saw a girl from Zimbabwe, they are sharing her, but I don't know whether she agreed or not. She is shared by the security. They share her like they want her. They promise her that if she agrees they will take her out. The day we wanted to go out they took out our photos. Then one guys said, if you love me stay here, I will take you out, I won't send you to

where you come from, you will go to where you stay now.
I didn't agree but I said, I won't do it, I said if you arrest
me I am going back to Malawi and won't go back again
(Participant 9).

Another Focus Group participant from Zimbabwe attempted to bribe
police in Johannesburg to avoid detention. When her bribe was turned
down, she was taken to Lindela, where she stated that detainees were
denied food, and were physically abused by officials:

> While I was staying [in Alexandra] I was always a victim for
> the police arrests and raids every time…. At times I would
> bribe them but at other times they turned down a bribe…. If
> we don't bribe them they'll take us with them to the police
> station. But what used to amaze me was that this was done
> by the same people every time and they knew us they would
> make us pay, one day found me alone and my friend was
> not there, they took me to Lindela where they kept me for
> two weeks and from there they took me home. I went back
> home and then I returned back here…. It depends on how
> you talk, sometimes [the police] can allow you not to go
> to Lindela or sometimes they refuse to take money from us
> and take us to Lindela. It's hard there, the securities beat us,
> and life there is just not good. We are sometimes denied to
> eat and sometimes we get it late and they give us little food
> and we're hungry. In accordance to me it's not right because
> every time I return from Lindela I will be very sick. We eat
> porridge. They give tea with milk already and you can't see
> if they have put something inside your tea, and a single slice
> of bread. And at three in the afternoon, they give us a little
> pap. That's all we eat. We do bathe [and] sleep but we have
> to share blankets yet we're sleeping on single separated beds.
> They have bedbugs (Focus Group 3, Participant 6).

Another woman thought that "pills" were added to the food at
Lindela. Suspicion about the food as a source of illness was also found by
the Ministerial Committee of Inquiry, particularly amongst Zimbabwean
migrants who were "concerned about deaths at the facility [and the] lack
of transparency on the part of Lindela and Consulates that represent the
interest of the ruling party in Zimbabwe." The Ministerial Committee
reported that organizations representing detained Zimbabweans "claim
that people detained are healthy but only contract illness after a few days
of their detention. Detainees are not availed to emergency medical care
and they suspect food as the cause of deaths…They pointed out that
there were people who were deported to Zimbabwe whilst on a criti-

cal state. Zimbabwean officials at the Beit Bridge Border Post have also raised concerns about strange patterns of illnesses."[40]

Whether or not such claims about the food at Lindela are well-founded, the Ministerial Committee found that the response to illness amongst detainees was inadequate. Detainees who were ill were only referred to the hospital "in late stages of illness (critically ill and terminal)" and as a result "70% of patients died within one day of arrival [at Leratong Hospital] with no opportunity for special investigations." The Committee also reported that patient histories were not recorded at Lindela or communicated to hospital staff, and that overcrowded conditions within the facility have led to the spread of Meningococcal Meningitis and other communicable diseases.[41]

A migrant in a Makhado Focus Group engaged in cross-border trade described how she was woken by police officers while sleeping at a station in Beitbridge. After police officers demanded to see her passport, declaration forms and the goods she was carrying, she was taken to the police station and asked to pay a bribe "so that we can be afraid and give them something." Although she paid R300, she was still taken to Lindela:

> [The police] came while we were sleeping and they asked
> for the passport and we showed them and everything we had
> and they said that we are going to our offices we went to
> their offices, and when we got there they said that each of
> us must pay R300 and we paid it and we stayed for five days
> and they took us to Lindela on the sixth day and we stayed
> at Lindela for seven days and they didn't mention what was
> the R300 for and we paid out of our own pockets. We had
> declared our goods and we had passports (Focus Group 5,
> Participant 2).

At Lindela, she was subjected to invasive body searches and deprived of food:

> We paid even if I had to go home, if you said that you did
> not have any money you just got here today, they would
> send a lady to search us and it was irritating and she wear
> gloves. Simply because we are hiding the money, we hide it
> in our private parts. Yes, this lady they got that R300 and
> there were about eleven of us and they didn't assist us with
> anything they left us to starve. They left us without food.
> We spent the whole six days without food, but they gave us
> a little bit porridge in the morning and a bit of pap and some
> vegetables, that's when they started to assess us according
> to our age. How old we were, so that they can transport
> us, the old would go with the old and the youth with the

youth because they were using a small van. From Lindela we used a small van to Beitbridge, from Beitbridge, some of the things were missing and some people lost they passports because they were holding our passports. The police, some when we told them that our things were missing they said that its not their fault (Focus Group 5 Participant 2).

TREATMENT AT HOSPITALS

Migrant women also frequently receive poor treatment from staff at clinics, hospitals and other health facilities. Women stated that they were often met with xenophobic attitudes, received substandard medical treatment, were over-charged for services, or were directly turned away from hospitals and clinics. A number of women viewed city hospitals in Johannesburg as the least likely to offer treatment to migrants.

One migrant participating in a Focus Group in Makhado said of hospital and clinic staff, "the first thing they say – makwerekwere" (Focus Group 6). A second Focus Group participant in Johannesburg described how hospitals express "prejudice" against foreigners:

What I know is that, if you are a foreigner other hospitals are prejudice against you. They don't treat you well as a person from this country. I have experienced this; this nurse was trying to get a fight with me. She told all those nurses that I was rude to her; even people from this country were rude to her, because she was rude to them, and they wanted to hit her. She treated me badly, but people didn't like what she was doing to me, and also the way she treated them. If they see that you're a foreigner it's worse (Focus Group 4, Participant 1).

Two women explained how they had been told to "go back to Zimbabwe" when seeking medical treatment at clinics:

It's like me when I go to the clinic. I went to the clinic and I had a headache, and when I got there the nurse asked me what was my problem and I told her that my head is aching and she said that why can't you go to Zimbabwe. Because I was sick I went there to seek help, but she told me to go to seek help at Zimbabwe, and I told her that I'm not here for holiday but I'm here because I'm sick. I told her that I did not come for politics. She just gave me some tablets and I left, she didn't even check my temperature or anything (Focus Group 5).

> I remember the last time I went to clinic and the other person said this one is from Zimbabwe she must go back to Zimbabwe you won't get any medicine. We give the South Africans only. This medicine is for South African only. They only gave me Panado even in the hospitals (Focus Group 6).

A Focus Group participant interviewed in Johannesburg said that nurses had refused to speak to her in English, and refused to attend to her until South African patients had been treated:

> When I was pregnant I went to the clinic and the nurses just said speak the South African accent. I was seven months pregnant and I went there not knowing only English, no other language, and they were saying this is South Africa speak our language. They didn't attend me and they didn't pay attention to me, and everyone they just passed by me and attending to other South Africans who are pregnant. And I went there early in the morning and I came there about two beds or something. They treated me but late, they did not pay attention to me. They came later on and say what are you saying now. It was my first time when I went to register my name at the clinic. They did attend to me well, but when I was giving birth they were very unfriendly (Focus Group 1, Participant 2).

A second Focus Group participant described how she had anticipated that she would have problems registering in advance for the birth of her child at Johannesburg hospitals. Instead, she decided to give birth at a medical facility in Chiawelo, Soweto. On admission she was met with a negative reaction from nurses:

> I only got a problem on the day that I was giving birth on. My nurse that was helping me, I think from Bophuthatswana or Lesotho, I'm not really sure. When I got inside the hospital she asked where I was from and why was I crying loudly? I told her I was from Mozambique. She said: "Mozambique? You came to South Africa and left Mozambican nurses sleeping back home and you chose to come and bother us here." She told me that I'll have to take care of myself and that she wasn't going to help me. You know, she tried to lie about me to the other nurses that came in – two nurses came in – they asked why I was sleeping on the floor? She told them that I was rude to her, how can you be disrespectful to a person if you're in pain. I was about to give birth and she took my baby to bath it. She came back with the baby and I told her that there was something I needed to tell her.

> I thanked her for helping me, because I almost died – I told
> her that this other nurse lied about me. All these stories she
> told you were all lies, she wanted me dead. These are those
> nurses that are cruel (Focus Group 4).

Again, her account of being told to "take care of myself" and "sleeping on the floor" before giving birth suggested dangerous levels of neglect, and a violation of the right of access to both reproductive and emergency health care.

A third migrant recounted how she had experienced similar treatment at a hospital where she was admitted while in labour:

> They refused to attend to me when I was in labour at the
> hospital. They were refusing, I was in red and the baby was
> coming out alone, I was crying alone, yes they left my baby
> alone.... They didn't assist me, and after they heard the
> baby crying, somebody came in quickly but I had already
> given birth by then.... It was very painful out there in the
> car. People from other countries treat me like we are sis-
> ters and brothers. Even in hospital they treat us bad. If we
> are not punctual they don't treat us, instead they insult
> us and say 'go away, makwerekwere'. They treat us bad in
> government hospitals. I want them to change their attitude
> because we are all Africans and black, we are all the same
> (Focus Group 3, Participant 3).

Experiences of neglect, inattention and maltreatment were common amongst migrant women admitted to hospitals and clinics to give birth. This was also the case for migrant women seeking treatment for serious illnesses and emergencies. One Focus Group participant described her experience of serious illness, later diagnosed as meningitis. She had waited for three hours at a clinic without being seen by a doctor or admitted to a bed, while South African patients were treated immediately after arriving. Eventually, she was told to leave the clinic because there was insufficient space to admit her (Focus Group 2, Participant 2).

A number of migrant women also suspected that they were overcharged when visiting public clinics and hospitals. Perceptions of overcharging were often complicated by difficulty in communicating with medical staff in English or other languages, and lack of understanding of public health care costing and billing structures:

> I won't go to register at Johannesburg Hospital.... Because
> at the time when I was supposed to register, I couldn't
> understand properly what they were saying. Firstly, when you
> go there, they want an I.D.... I don't have. I use my passport

and my passport is at home, you see? The next thing I have to go to Rand clinic and at that clinic they make you pay, you see? Or I'll go to a doctor and I'll have to pay, like now if you want to give birth they charge R1200 ... for me to be able to deliver a baby since I don't have a passport or a ID (Focus Group 4, Participant 8).

Sometimes they treat us bad, especially in clinics when you are sick. I was sick so I went to the Johannesburg Hospital. I asked them to help me but they asked me to show them an ID and a passport, they said I must pay. I had to pay R1500 to have a file and to be treated.... I told them I don't have that kind of money, so they didn't treat me. I returned the next week – they told me the same thing, I told them I don't have money, I work in the streets doing hair.... If you are a foreigner going to the hospital, they treat you badly (Participant 12).

These texts highlight a particular problem for migrant women in South Africa. While many are legally and constitutionally entitled to access health care and cannot be denied emergency medical treatment, those who are either undocumented, casually employed or working in the informal sector are unable to verify their status in South Africa or provide proof of their level of income. As a result, women migrants are unable to qualify for low-cost medical treatment or meet prohibitive costs at private clinics, and therefore often go without basic health care.

Migrant women also encountered a number of other barriers to accessing adequate medical care in South Africa. For a migrant farm worker participating in a Makhado Focus Group, these barriers included unfair treatment by her employer, distrust of the police, and fear of arrest and deportation. She described two pregnancies in South Africa, and losing both babies as a result of lack of access to medical treatment:

I went to [a farm], I found a guy there I fell in love with him and I was pregnant with his child and I was working, it was nine months and I felt labour pains and I told the foreman and he told his boss that this woman needs to go to the clinic, then the boss said that not today but tomorrow.... I don't know [why they said that], maybe the boss didn't like me to go to hospital, it was during the month and I did have money or maybe the foreman asked him for money, but he gave the foreman the bakkie to take me to the compound and he took me there and he left me there, to give birth to a child alone. It was in the placenta, I did not know how to tear off that thing.

Without any assistance, I gave birth to the child – it was bleeding and after two hours it died because I didn't know what to do. So the foreman told his boss and the boss called the police and they asked me that I wanted to abort. I said no, I told them that I told the boss that I wanted to go to the hospital but he said tomorrow, and the boss refused that he said that, so the police said that if we find that you were trying to abort the child we are going to arrest you. Then the boss took me to the clinic and they checked me and they found that I didn't do nothing wrong, they send me back to the compound, during the month they gave me my salary and told me that the work is over.

The police got there and found the baby and said that its not their job, they called the emergency service when they got there also they said that its not their job this is for undertaker then from there I don't know what happened to the baby.

[At the] Hotel, where I got again pregnant, at six months I was in town I got in a bus and felt pains then I told someone that I'm pregnant and I'm having pains in my stomach, the person shouted I was furious, so he told the driver to drive a little bit faster and when we got to the King Korn some go out and found help, they took me out of the bus and then I had my miscarriage, I was afraid of the police. Because the people that I worked with told me that I don't have a passport I should not go to the hospital I will get arrested, that's why I had a miscarriage along the N1 and the police came and asked what happened and my madam told that I had a miscarriage and the older women came and throw the baby away just like that … it was my madam who told that woman to do that. I was shivering, the madam took me to the compound and gave a glass of water and a bath and she told me time so that I could rest, when I'm feeling better we can go to the hospital (Participant 5, Focus Group 5).

News of the neglect and poor treatment of foreign women in South African clinics and hospitals has spread quickly within migrant communities. Many women were deeply suspicious and fearful of medical treatment and institutions in South Africa. Rumours fly and are believed:

If you're not a South African you lose your baby (Focus Group 4, Participant 1).

> The children are being murdered there [in the hospital]. I heard that at the Johannesburg Hospital they give the babies their injections with a dirty needle, after you have given birth. And secondly they switch the babies, if you are not careful they swap the babies around. I'm telling you this, because I've been to hospital and I've heard people from South Africa talking about it. And they are given dirty injections; it's even better if you give birth outside the country, outsider – after 2 or 3 months you may lose your baby.... I didn't hear it from outside people I heard it from people that belong to this country. I didn't register, because I don't have an ID ... but this I heard South Africans that have registered. They say you should be careful, because the nurses are in a conspiracy.... South Africans said this and not a foreigner. They are talking about something that happens in hospitals. They want to know why babies are given dirty injection and why babies are swap around. They say you should be careful after giving birth; South African women spoke all this (Focus Group 4).

TREATMENT AS WOMEN

MVP participants also endured gendered discrimination and abuse in South Africa in a number of different ways.

Although most participants felt that men and women are generally treated "the same" in South Africa, interview texts revealed gendered differences in women's experiences. Women were certainly seen as more vulnerable to crime:

> I think the government doesn't [have] any issues with anybody who's got their papers. Okay, as the human being outside in the community, if you're a man the people are always scared of you, so I think if you are a man your life is much easier because if you walk in the street you're not scared of anybody. But when I walk around Hillbrow I always think, what if somebody grabs me and shoves me into a dark place and rapes me and things like that ... what if these men – hmmmm, coming towards me. What if he takes my phone or rapes me or kills me for no reason (Participant 19).

While male migrants in South Africa might be equally fearful of vulnerability to crime, one participant suggested that "if you are a man your life is much easier" because "you're not scared of anybody."

Women also feel more vulnerable to crime in South Africa than in their countries of origin:

> Crime, it's easy, anyone has a gun here, even different from our countries, they come to us and say that you are kwere-kwere, you can't do nothing to us even we kill you, it's okay because we are kwere-kwere.... Foreigners can't report crime because they are afraid (Focus Group 2, Participant 1).

> In Zimbabwe rape cases are there but they're not much, they are not that high. It's three times rare to hear somebody has been raped but here you always hear rape times four, you see, and people shooting, they are always scared of those things (Participant 19).

Migrant women's fears of vulnerability to crime were compounded by distrust of police officers. Women also discussed a higher level of distrust towards men in South Africa than in their countries of origin. A migrant from Zimbabwe stated that she is now "afraid men are thieves" and that migrant women "can't welcome a man because you are afraid" (Participant 47).

With most of the interview participants describing themselves as "single," discussion of gendered differences in migration experiences also led women to talk about their own relationships. Many of the women described a desire to find partners and enter into long-term relationships. This was particularly true of long-term migrants intending to stay in South Africa on a permanent basis. Several women were wary of casual relationships, and one Focus Group participant asked, "We are stranded here, what about us? What are we going to do, because you can't just go to anywhere and sleep with anyone?" A migrant participating in the same Focus Group added concerns about AIDS and other sexually transmitted infections, cautioning that it is "very difficult now to just sleep with other men, there's AIDS.... You can catch [infections] and you die what will happen to your children?" (Focus Group 5).

Women were clearly frustrated by perceptions amongst South Africans that they would try to "steal" husbands or marry citizens solely to obtain residence.

One Makhado Focus Group participant said that foreign men and women are both blamed for the same thing: "These things about relationships is funny because the South African women are saying Nigerians are taking our man as much as Nigerians are complaining that South Africans are taking their man, but I think it doesn't matter, it is matter of how you take it" (Focus Group 6).

Some of the women did not differentiate between South Africans and men of other nationalities as potential partners. Women in a Makhado

Focus Group suggested that relationships are "a matter of how you take it" that "has to do with what you are looking for in a partner," so it "doesn't matter whether your partner is a South African or wherever" (Focus Group 6). A Johannesburg Focus Group participant agreed that the quality of a relationship was not determined by individual nationality:

> [Men] are all the same if he can trust you and you trust him then this will work, I know that men are the same – they just want trust. It does not matter where is the guy from as long as you love him its good, because he can say that he is not married while he is so you will never know better love from the person (Focus Group 2, Participant 6).

Other migrant women were more wary of South African men:

> Most [South African men] they just want to marry Zimbabwean women, at the end of the day South African men, they say that [Zimbabwean women] are well behaved and work hard. It's true (Focus Group 5).

> It depends what type of guy is he, some of these guys take chances – like Zimbabweans, they say the women from that side are soft – if you stay with him after 2 months he will start getting funny when you ask they will fight you. They are all not trustworthy. South African guys know how to abuse women (Focus Group 2, Participant 5).

> Men in South Africa are jealous and they use guns, back home its different – men, they use a s'jambock (Focus Group 2, Participant 1).

> [South African men] will also beat you up. South African men are abusive. They are rough. Yes. They don't [mess] around they'll hit you. They take the beer bottle and hit you with it and they don't miss. [Men from other countries also hit you], but not as South Africans (Focus Group 4, Participant 5).

> [Men from other countries] don't know how to use weapons. He'll show you a knife and tell you that he'll stab the living day lights out of you. It's hard for men [from other countries] to do that. I usually listen to the radio and hear how women abuse is high, I listen to the news on the radio and South Africa has a high rate of women abuse. This year already I've heard 3 stories of men who have killed their wives and kids with guns. He will shoot his wife and child;

he'll even kill his own mother-in-law. Things like that you see? (Focus Group 4).

Migrant women expressed a number of other fears related to relationships with South African men, primarily around potential loss of independence, loss of material goods or assets, and the difficulty of overcoming cultural differences. A Focus Group participant who feared a South African partner would limit her access to her family and children in Zimbabwe preferred to start a relationship with a partner who was also a migrant:

> [My boyfriend] is from that other side. It's because I've got kids in Zimbabwe, so if I get a boyfriend here in South Africa, he'll force me to go and stay at his home and my kids will starve, from how I view it (Focus Group 5).

A second woman felt that she would be unable to follow the different cultural "rules" imposed by a South African husband:

> You find that South African men have too many rules. Rules that you won't understand, like that you shouldn't work, go outside or he'll just give you too many rules just because you're married (Focus Group 4, Participant 8).

Several other migrants suspected that, once in a relationship, a South African man might easily revert to the xenophobic attitudes and behaviours of other citizens:

> It's hard to get married here. We are scared to get married to South Africans. Let me say that, I'm scared of getting married to a South African, because I think that once you're married to him he might turn and say you're not from here, you're a kwere-kwere from Zimbabwe (Focus Group 4).

They also feared that South African partners or husbands could easily take advantage of them if relationships broke down:

> Maybe when we're married and had bought [property] – he'll tell you to leave and go back to Zimbabwe and not take anything. Or that you're using his name to stay here permanently and get married. Suppose, maybe you're working. You sell right, even if it's at the streets, that money will help you buy food in the house. You buy things for the house with that money. And when he doesn't want you anymore, he'll chase you out and tell you that you're a kwere-kwere. So, those are the – you'll never get your things. Yes, you're a kwere-kwere, right? So, you'll get nothing (Focus Group 4).

Many migrant women said that they preferred to be in relationships with non-South Africans for as one stated, "we prefer our own." These preferences were again linked to negative perceptions about South African men, and stories of physical abuse. As a Malawian Focus Group participant commented, "The kwere-kweres are far, much better – they are caring and loving" (Focus Group 4, Participant 5).

Some women migrants also prefer partners from similar cultural backgrounds to their own, and who share similar social norms and values. One Focus Group participant explained that she preferred to have relationships with other Zimbabweans because "they know me and they will know how to treat me the rules and the culture" (Focus Group 2). Relationships with men of the same nationality or of a shared cultural background allowed migrant women the sense that they could better predict gendered roles and behaviours. For some women, male behaviours and gender roles that were negative, but predictable, were preferable to the "foreign" and seemingly unpredictable territory of relationships with South African men. One woman who described how "in Mozambique they think that a woman should be beaten up" still preferred relationships with Mozambican men rather than South Africans:

> People from Mozambique don't [use weapons to abuse women]. They only have one fault and that is that they love women. Mozambican men love women. They can date two women from the same street at the same time. Even where we sell, they can date two different women from the same spot that we sell at. Mozambican women are strict; we cook, clean and do the laundry for your man. And we do the household chores so that when he arrives he'll find that everything is in good shape. But! They follow this tradition that a woman is a woman; if I want to I can stop her. People from our country – in Mozambique, they think that a woman should be beaten up. You should obey them all the time, as he is the one who provides, you should ask him for everything. He will harass you, because he's the breadwinner of the family. But they don't use weapons or things to hit you with. They don't usually do that (Focus Group 4 Participant 4).

A second Mozambican migrant participating in the same Focus Group discussion challenged any tolerance of physical abuse on the basis of shared nationality or culture. At the same time, she pointed out that migrant women have little recourse to report abuse to police in South Africa:

> Mozambican women have a problem with our men. These

men like to fetch us from Mozambique and bring us here. While you're here he'd give you problems, sometimes he hits you or tells you that you should go outside. You shouldn't go to the shop. You actually go nowhere. You see? Sometimes if this man gives you problems we get scared to go to the police, because we're scared that they'll arrest us. We get scared to go to the police station. We're scared of our husbands. I'm not scared to go to the police station to report a person that has done me wrong. But their husbands that fetch them in Mozambique to bring them here give women from Mozambique problems. They are scared to go to the police station to report any crimes. They say they are scared that they'll arrest them (Focus Group 4 Participant 3).

IMPORTANCE OF MIGRATION FOR WOMEN IN SADC

Beyond the individual experiences of participants, the MVP study also sought to assess how "important" migrants think that migration is for women in the region overall. Most felt that migration is extremely important in the region, particularly for women. The importance of migration was most often linked to the economic benefits accrued by migrant women and their families, but other benefits included access to education, opportunities for training and skills development and exposure to different cultures.

Given that many of the women interviewed had been "pushed" to migrate by factors such as poverty and hardship and had experienced improvements in income levels and quality of life after migrating, migrant women often link the importance of migration to economic opportunity. Many emphasized the significance of being able to support and provide for children and extended families.

In several cases, migration was viewed as an important economic strategy for women who had become primary household breadwinners in the absence of male partners:

> [Migration is] very important, like me I am not married, I have to look after my kids, so ladies have to work for themselves if you are divorced or single, you have to work for your kid and your family (Participant 34).

> It is important because we support our children because some of us, our men leave us – they go away. So you won't just sit down and wait for your man to come back because things get worse. You have to be able to feed your children because when your baby grow without a father it is not right

– that thing hurts. Other women are able to go up and down so that they can support their children and educate them because a person won't be able to grow without going to school. What kind of future would that person have because his father wasn't there, so the baby must not go to crèche or school? Even us women, we have to fight because we know what we want, we don't have to depend on men (Participant 9).

Other interview participants suggested that, with or without male partners, women in the region would continue to assume primary responsibility for supporting households and families. Migration was therefore viewed as a strategy for women to "stand up and do things for themselves" and to better fulfil their supportive roles in the family:

If their families are in need they must stand up, and they must do something, do themselves for a change. Gone are the days when you would just sit and expect men to feed you, you have got to do it for yourself sometimes (Participant 54).

Women are the ones who take care of their families most of the time. Because women know that my family has to bathe, eat and get some clothing, but men don't care for a family. It is important for women to stand and do things for themselves (Participant 28).

Yes, [it is important for women to migrate] because they are the ones who are responsible at home. They are the ones who support the family. [Men] do, but women are the ones that work harder (Participant 24).

Other men when they are here they don't do what they came here for, they get married, they forget about their kids, and they won't see if you are suffering at home, that's why I say you have to make a plan as a woman. [The experiences of men and women] are different because we are the ones who give birth and if you have a family or children you are the one responsible for those children, but man, when they come here they do this and that and they forget about their children. As I am sitting here I am making money for my children and if the stock is finished I go back home but everything I need I buy it in my house, but women do this and that, you can see that the experience is not the same from that of man (Participant 40).

A woman has more brains than man. A man can just leave his wife home and come this side and sit and just forget. Maybe you will be sitting at home and then next thing your husband has another wife in Johannesburg, but a woman will come to Johannesburg and still think of going back home to her children…. A man can stay here for 10 years without returning home. We just wait for him, what will we do? He would say, "Can't you hear when I say where I work from there are no phones?" And when you are just a woman and maybe you are in the rural area there is nothing like phones. He will tell you that you don't have to write him a letter 'cause once you do that he'll be arrested. So you just stay at home and wait (Participant 28).

For women already situated in gendered "caring" roles within households, the additional responsibility of becoming a main breadwinner could potentially have been viewed as burdensome. However, many participants instead underscored the increased economic and personal independence they gained through migration.

Beyond its economic benefits, participants suggested that the experience of migration was important for women in the region for a number of other reasons. A number placed a high value on the experience of travel itself; a positive feature of migration widely recognized amongst wealthier travellers and tourists but often overlooked in relation to poor migrants:

Yes, [migration] is important. Do you think it is nice to be a lazy mother and never know other countries because you will find yourself in a difficult situation when a person ask you to come to South Africa, Botswana or UK, you wouldn't know what to do. You wouldn't know what to do at the border or which forms do you have to fill or what (Participant 23).

It is very important because if you migrate you get exposure to new ideas, you know if you stay in Zimbabwe, Zimbabwe is a closed country to you, things like internet and these latest technology, in Zimbabwe they come very late, so if you migrate you become open-minded (Participant 69).

It's important to me because now I've experienced a lot in traveling from one country to another, I know so many things, I've experienced so many things and the good thing is that I now know different cultures, we are just a little bit different, but otherwise we Africans are just the same … if I weren't enjoying it, I wouldn't be here now. I'm very

> free, I've learnt so many languages, I only used to speak
> my mother tongue but now I know a little bit of seSotho,
> seTswana, isiXhosa, isiZulu and etc. So it's very interesting,
> even though I did it to earn money, but now I'm okay, and if
> I can skip a month without coming here, I feel like there is
> something incomplete in me (Participant 46).

Others suggested that through migration, women in the region were able to access increased opportunities for education, skills development, and entrepreneurship:

> It is important because we learn lots of things, because in
> our countries we are not business-oriented, but when you
> see women here working, you learn to work. It's important
> for women to migrate because they learn lots of things that
> have a meaning in life. You learn a lot of different things,
> because when I arrived in this country I discovered that
> there are lots of women that work and sell things when they
> knock off work. So I learned that I could work and sell too,
> at the same time (Participant 37).

> Because when you are poor you decide to leave and go to
> other countries. When you are at home you see others who
> are poor and others you are not even friends with. So it's
> better you move away from them and see other people with
> different ideas (Participant 8).

> It is so important for women [to travel] because they are
> contributing to the society, according to my view, they are
> best future planners as compared to men, and they achieve
> more skills that they didn't have and they pass them on
> to others. It increases women's status because they are of
> the civilized new generation women, and they are not like
> women from the ancient days who used to stay at home
> and expect their husbands to work for them.... Migration
> is important because we migrate for different reasons, some
> migrate because of their situations at home, some to do
> things that they are not able to do when they are at their
> home country, and some migrate to further their studies
> because they can't learn what they desire in their own coun-
> tries (Participant 2).

IS MIGRATION EASIER FOR WOMEN OR MEN?

P articipants were asked how easy it is for women to migrate in the region. Notably, in spite of the difficulties they encountered, many participants felt that migration is "easy" for women in the region. Migration is viewed as "easier" for women than men amongst some participants. Most often this was explained through a number of gendered social characteristics attributed to women migrants. First, women migrants are simply more "likeable" than men, making it easier to negotiate social interactions during migration:

> Women's experiences are different from those of men to
> some extent. Many people will help or assist a woman first,
> some as a mother, some as a sister, some as a mother-in-law
> (Participant 56).

Participants also suggested that women migrants are less likely than men to be viewed with suspicion, particularly by officials at border posts:

> I don't think it's difficult because when you arrive at the
> border gate they check visa and the things you have, then
> you enter – for the men it's very difficult, unlike women
> are not normally suspected but men are always suspected
> (Participant 10).

> The ladies are never treated badly but the guys are treated
> badly. I can say that again they view men as potential crimi-
> nals and the ladies just as partners (Participant 57).

In these cases, gender was viewed as an advantage for women migrants, rather than a source of increased vulnerability.

Second, in addition to "likeable" and "trustworthy" qualities, partici-
pants suggested that women are better able to "talk" or "speak" and be understood by others than male migrants:

> For a woman it is not difficult. I know when a woman speaks
> she can be heard but for a man it is scarce (Long Malawi
> 63).

> We can talk – man can't do anything, you know, like
> women. Sometimes man fail to talk to officers, they say what
> can we do (Participant 47).

> I don't know how to say this – it's because us women, the
> thing that God gave us, I don't know if it is luck or what,
> because sometimes we talk to man and they understand us,
> but a man talking to another man, they don't understand

each other. You find that they need money and a man won't take out his money, and then they will fight, but us woman, when a person ask for money and you say you don't have money and then ask for their sympathy and explain that you have children to support and a house and everything and I am the only one and I don't have a man (Participant 9).

A third, and unanticipated advantage for women migrants was the ability to "remember" family members left behind in countries of origin. A number of participants said male migrants had a tendency to "forget" partners, children and families. The tendency of male migrants to "come this side and sit and just forget" may be linked to historical patterns of traditionally male labour migration in Southern Africa, which led to pro-tracted absences by male household heads.[42] One woman from Zimbabwe noted that:

If we can take a man to come here he can be able to work and spend all his money or marry another woman, but a woman is able to remember that she left her children at home. The woman can be able to work and raise her chil-dren, support them, educate them and so forth. As a woman I didn't face any problems and I didn't see any, as long as your documents are right I don't see what problems they can face (Participant 29).

The view that men were in a sense disadvantaged by a lesser obliga-tion towards family, or the inability to understand the needs of those left behind, challenges the idea that women migrants feel hindered by dependants and family commitments. The perception that women were actually "advantaged" by connections to their family and children under-scores a number of gender-specific "skills" and capabilities, such as the capacity to assume income-generating productive roles, and the repro-ductive roles of parenting and caregiving. These comments also highlight women's independence as actors in deciding to migrate and in migration processes.

At the same time, women identified a number of gendered obstacles to migration, including limited access to resources and opportunities, more extensive household and family responsibilities, and vulnerability to unequal treatment, discrimination and harassment. First, some said that women migrants are less able to access employment and jobs than men because, according to one, women are "not able to stay for a long time." Others felt that employers were more likely to hire male than female migrants:

I think it is difficult. It's because if you are a woman you are not like a man. You find that I am looking for a job but

I can't find it but the jobs that I find they need man and it becomes difficult for me, it is not the same, it is different (Participant 13).

They are different. Especially on the issue of work because men gets more jobs than women. Yes, it's difficult because they want to you to be educated. When you are educated it's much better (Participant 8).

Second, several participants commented that migration was ultimately easier for men because of reduced responsibilities at home:

Yes, it's different because we women are here because we seek survival for our kids to eat. But with men, they come this side and tend to forget about their kids, entertainments of this country excite them (Participant 15).

If I were a man other men wouldn't be happy with me but I would be popular with girls. I know that I wouldn't get along with men but I would get along with women.... It's because women have the experience, they are able to know when they do things they will get that, they don't think if they use this money for that they will get this, and this money will help them to get this thing, but a female person know that if I buy this bread and sell it like it will generate for me this money and I will be able to buy shoes, panties and trousers for my child. Maybe my child is at school and he pays R150, maybe if I am selling trousers my child can be able to pay school fees with half of the amount, but a man sometimes he does think and sometimes he doesn't think (Participant 9).

Third, some women migrants also felt they were more vulnerable to discrimination, harassment and abuse when traveling in the region:

They wouldn't treat me this way because you'll get scared of a man. You find another, the drivers are not the same, the other one shouts and one day I nearly fought with another driver in the taxis. You find that we are getting bored and we are traveling long distance, maybe I have my cassette and ask, brother will you please play me the cassette, and it start right then. A man won't shout at another man, they shout at us because we are woman but they won't shout at men. We don't have the power to fight with them (Participant 6).

We don't have power us women. The problem I normally see is that I personally speak to anyone anyway for anyone to hear me, stating that now it is 50-50 because I have no power. When you are traveling alone it is hard (Participant 21).

Women sacrifice a lot along the way. There is a lot of abuse. Abuse from people who ask favour, and all those things. When she is asking for a lift, the driver will demand something from the women rather than giving a ride free of charge … these are some of the things that women get exposed to. And generally the harassment, the police harassment. You find that women, they are being harassed left and right. And they are women, they cannot defend themselves, cannot speak for themselves, they are endangered you know, they do not have a choice. But they would have to accept anything (Participant 71).

GENDER CHALLENGES WOMEN FACE

Participants identified a number of gender-specific obstacles and challenges for women migrating in the region, and many of these related to the logistics and practicalities of travel. Most fundamentally, participants acknowledged the actual cost of migration, stating that it is "easy if you have money to migrate" (Participant 12) and that "money matters most" (Participant 63). Several participants discussed the need for money in the context of efforts to travel legally, and meeting migration requirements including visas and "sufficient available financial resources"[43] necessary to enter South Africa:

It's difficult because you have to pay and if you have a big family you pay lots of money and you find that person does not get paid well. So that is why when you want to visit there you must prepare a passport, visa and prepare money and things you are going to buy and to take with you. I think it's good [to have a visa and passport] because you don't have to travel by foot and you won't enter the border by jumping fences. You will enter properly. Sometimes it's not easy because you pay a lot of money (Participant 10)

It is not easy for women because migrating from region to region, it is difficult, you have to have a certain amount of money and that amount of money they want to see it in the bank. They are specific. Like when I come from Zimbabwe I want to come this side, you have to have at least R1000, which they want to see it. If you don't have that money they can turn you back (Participant 43).

Yes they say you must have money to enter and pay hotels. We can't afford it because we are poor. I can't get that money, that's why I sell doilies. Yes, it's difficult sometimes they want R2000 for you to enter this side. So that I can't afford to pay a hotel to my side, I can't pay that money, it will be too much if they make that law (Participant 49).

Participants also discussed the need for money in order to pay bribes to the police, as described by a long-term migrant from Zimbabwe:

It was difficult to travel from one country to another – people use different money, currencies, you come from the country with dollars and South Africa you use Rands.... It is difficult for us to travel on our way, especially us girls, for example man have money and when they come across police they have money to bribe but we don't – money, where can we get money. It is difficult to move away from your home (Participant 21).

Given that many participants were household heads seeking livelihoods to support children and other dependent family members, access to money was viewed as an obstacle to migration particularly impacting on women.

The participants suggested that a further obstacle for women migrants who are able to access and save the money necessary to travel is transportation which, linked to concerns about the cost of migration, was viewed as overly unaffordable. A long-term migrant from Lesotho who stated that she wasn't aware of difficulties experienced by women migrating in the region nonetheless acknowledged that "transport might be a problem because it's expensive, they spend a lot on transport" (Participant 5). This was a particular problem for women involved in small-scale cross-border trade with limited profit margins, as described by a male interview participant from Zimbabwe:

The problems that affect women is how to raise the money – bus fares are going up every day and the things that we, the goods we buy to come and sell, also arranging the amount is becoming too much and the duties that we are being charged also, so spend a lot in just one day which, when you come here you don't just come here, you don't sell your things at one place. That means when you reach the Park Station either I'm going to Rustenberg or I am going to Klerksdorp to sell my things there, but now you can find the profit now you end up nowhere because the expense is too much (Male Zim 4).

Participants also raised concerns about the safety of transportation for women migrants, referring to both "road accidents, and you might think that you can be involved in one of those accidents" (Participant 5), and vulnerability to abuse. As described by a male interview participant from South Africa, "most of the times the people who drive, the people who drive cars or trucks" are men, and "us men are known to have to take advantage of women, if you see you talk to them, they are vulnerable, they don't have places to stay, things like that" (Participant 62).

A third, practical obstacle for women migrants was finding suitable accommodation. Participants commented that sometimes women migrants "do not have a place to stay" (Participant 33) and that suitable accommodation is "what they need most" (Participant 15), and again emphasized concerns over both cost and safety:

> I want to stay if I come to this place, I don't have a place
> to stay because I pay R50 every week, R50 every week not
> every month, so it is difficult (Participant 48).

> If you're a woman, when you arrive there is no place to go,
> there is no place and then they aren't any people you know,
> there are thieves, and we don't know where to stay. At least
> if you're a man is better, because you're able to survive; you
> are able to maintain yourself (Participant 3).

A Key Informant working as a bus driver added that migrant women arriving in the country to "sell their stuff" are often "stranded to get accommodation," and as a result sometimes have to "sleep in the open area" (Participant 73).

In addition to specific concerns raised around transportation and accommodation, safety risks were viewed as amongst the most significant obstacles to migration for women traveling within the SADC region. In this respect, participants emphasized significant differences in the experiences of male and female migrants:

> [The experiences] don't differ that much but in terms of
> safety women are more of an easy target than men. It can be
> rape or being robbed (Participant 1).

> No, it's not the same [for men and women], sometimes
> women can be hurt, that is abuse, it can be lot actually,
> woman doesn't carry a gun, doesn't do anything (Participant
> 7).

Participants also commented on the disproportionate vulnerability of women migrants to harassment, abuse and rape during the migration process:

It's hard on women because a woman has strength more than a man and because many women we see them here selling clothes but the men are few. No, it's not the same [for men and women]. Women experience lots of heartache. It's hard because they get abused on the way, they are raped and also when they arrive here, they don't live happy here. They are here to sell (Participant 32).

It is not easy for women to migrate from one country to another. Because women are abused sometimes by their bosses. Yes, even by their bus drivers and the taxi drivers (Participant 18).

We pay money, sometimes you pay money but they arrest you. Sometimes they take you back home but sometimes they rape you in the bushes. Sometimes the police beat you up and send the dogs to bite you like that (Participant 9).

However, consistent with their own experiences in many cases, participants also emphasized the particular dangers of "risky" (Participant 5, 25) irregular border crossings.

Safety risks and crime were also identified by male participants as the foremost challenges faced by women migrants, with interview texts focusing particularly on women's vulnerability to abuse and crime at the hands of tsotsis, thugs, and even "security" officers (Participant 68). Similar to the women migrants interviewed, male participants underscored the added risks of irregular border crossings:

I can say that most of these women come here, they don't use passports but they cross the border illegally through going through the national reserve parks and there, they meet thugs who rob and even rape them, so they are risking. Their journey to South Africa is not safe but they still insist to take it because of the situation they are facing. Men are the thugs that I'm talking about. You'll find that the person is deported and when they leave him there he would want to come back but has no money to return back, he will then decide to create a job for himself by mugging these women who are crossing the border illegally (Participant 63).

For a woman it is very difficult because from Zimbabwe you will be traveling without documents if you are not there the visa is very difficult to get, and if you try to migrate illegally sometimes you get robbed on the way and stuff so, it's difficult for a woman.... Obviously they use these cheap line of transport, they are always abused by the taxi drivers on their way migrating, officers they always shout at you, you know, so (Participant 69).

It is not easy, it is a hard task for instance if you travel from Zimbabwe and you don't have a passport or papers some of them as far as I have heard, they have to cross rivers which is not safe. We hear of these things that some of them they don't even make it there and some of them are being eaten by crocodiles in the Limpopo River. It is not easy – it's easy when you've got your papers right with you, then you can go through the borders but if you don't have it becomes difficult.... There may be a lot of them, you see on the way there are man who are brutal, some of them they get raped, abused and taken as sex slaves, it is not easy for woman in that extent (Participant 28).

However, several male participants also viewed men as advantaged by a number of gendered-assigned characteristics, including that "men are brave" and are able to "take any risk" (Participant 28), they "can easily cope with every tough circumstances" (Participant 65), and that they are able to "survive tough times" (Participant 62). One male participant from South Africa qualified these characteristics by stating, "I can just go to another country, I can sleep in a bar, I can drink until sunrise" (Participant 62). This was in contrast with depictions of women as "vulnerable," "not tough people" and "easily manipulated by unscrupulous people" (Participant 62, 65). A male participant from Swaziland also suggested that women "easily give in to the situation which might end up leaving them exposed to abuse." Beyond reasons given for vulnerability to crime, a male interview participant commented that safety risks faced by women migrants are significant, and commented that women's migration experiences "should be researched" (Participant 67).

Many of the challenges and obstacles identified as particularly impacting on women migrants related to practical and logistical barriers, including access to money, transportation and accommodation. However, women migrants in the region identified leaving family and children behind in countries of origin as one of the most difficult aspects of migration. As described by three long-term migrants from Zimbabwe:

As a woman I don't think is easy to leave home, especially for those who got kids at home. I think it is so difficult leaving the kids behind, but then again the situation forces you because you can't, there is no need for your kids every night and day and seeing them go hungry (Participant 19).

It is not easy because your family is at home and you are here. Yes, it is hard to move from home to here because it takes some time for you to see your family. Then you can see that it is not easy (Participant 20)

For a woman it is difficult. Because from her country to another country she leaves because she can't take it anymore. So she will be in need of money but as she needs money she will think that she has to go back to look for her children (Participant 28).

A number of male and female participants viewed leaving family and children behind in countries of origin as more difficult for women migrants than for men:

The experiences are different because women get close to their children so like if you have to make that decision, really a big step that you will be making, it's the decisions that you have to think twice, but for a man, always men from way back, they always been migrating, so it is easy for men. It's home, when you leaving home you know (Participant 69).

Yes, [migration experiences] do differ because when we are together we can be able to do something because a man doesn't think of doing anything. We know that a home is a home because of woman, because women know what are the needs of the family (Participant 20)

However, the challenge of leaving children and family behind in countries of origin was viewed as unavoidable for women migrants looking for work and other economic opportunities.

LEGAL AND POLICY CHALLENGES

The participants also identified a number of specific challenges faced by women migrants related to migration laws and policies in South Africa, as well as other countries in the region. Most of these challenges related to difficulties obtaining visas and IDs, as well as to foreign exchange and Customs practices at borders.

Relatively few participants viewed obtaining a passport as a major challenge for women migrants in the region. One exception to this was a long-term migrant from Swaziland, who commented that the "problem is the passport price, they can't afford it." She added that this price might prevent South African women from visiting Swaziland:

> I belong here and people want to go to Swaziland. The prob-
> lem is the passport price, they can't afford it. By the time
> I obtained it, it was R105, it is expensive and I want them
> to go and see how is Swaziland, the culture and tradition,
> especially during the ceremony where the king get to choose
> a girl to be his wife. If you can go visit our country, see the
> lifestyle and culture. It would be nice for women here to
> go and teach the women there their handicraft and learn
> theirs. Women in Swaziland are great designers and it could
> be better to exchange designs with women in South Africa
> (Participant 16).

A second long-term migrant also described having "troubles" after she lost her passport in South Africa (Participant 25). However, in terms of documentation, participants viewed the need for IDs as far more challenging for women migrants, particularly in South Africa. Participants without IDs in South Africa discussed difficulties in finding work, as well as in opening bank accounts and obtaining credit. At the same time, most participants were likely to be ineligible to apply for South African IDs, by virtue of their temporary status in the country.

Obtaining visas to enter South Africa was viewed as a far greater obstacle for women migrants in the region; however, problems getting visas were discussed almost exclusively by Zimbabwean partici-pants, as countries in the region including Botswana, Malawi, Lesotho, Mozambique, Namibia, Swaziland, and Zambia are exempt from visa requirements for visitors entering South Africa for pre-defined time peri-ods. The participants generally viewed the process of obtaining a visa as difficult, lengthy and expensive:

> Talking from my country because here people get visas eas-
> ily because it is hard to get a visa in our country.... You
> know when you are a woman and migrating it is difficult
> (Participant 22).

> It is difficult, especially in the Zimbabwe side, because the
> visa takes a long time to be processed. Sometimes it can take
> on to two months, you have to pay R1000 to get the visa.
> You have to have it in Zimbabwe, you have to buy a travel-
> ler's cheque to show them, without R1000 you cannot get a
> visa (Participant 73).

The difficulty of obtaining a visa in Zimbabwe was linked by some participants to women's decisions to use the "border jumping method," rather than traveling through regular and legal means:

> These laws they make it too difficult for us to come this side,

that is why we are using border jumping method, it is the best method because with a visa, there are too many rules with the visa (Participant 34).

The most common complaint was that South African visas are simply too expensive for Zimbabweans, in terms of both actual cost and the "sufficient funds" required to qualify:

You know what they said in Zimbabwe – you must put visa that money, you must work hard to get money for visa so they must not do it that you must put visa, that one is very expensive (Participant 47).

Suppose you must have a passport and a visa and it's hard to get a visa because it's too expensive there in Zimbabwe. It's like one million and you suppose to have money in the bank account you see, so some are like me, they are not working so it was hard for me because my mother wasn't working. So you supposed to have money (Participant 30)

A number of participants, both male and female, also commented on how the high cost of visas is unaffordable for poor women in particular:

Most women in Zimbabwe don't have traveling documents so they decide to migrate, they have to start organizing their papers ... so it's one of the difficulties that they experience and sometimes you need a collateral to get a visa and you understand, so you so you need thousand Rand to get a visa so for women it's a disadvantage for a long time, they don't have that advantage (Participant 69).

Yes, it was difficult because South Africa want a visa from when you come from Zimbabwe. So to have a visa you need to have money. So I couldn't because I didn't have money. So that's what makes us end up thinking of – I think the last time it was R1000.... It is difficult because women can't follow it. So you find that they risk their lives because they want to cross and come this side. You find that some even swim through Limpopo River and get eaten by crocodiles when they come. Some of them die in the river because they want to come to this side. So I think it is difficult at least if there were no visas it was going to be easy. Visa makes people suffer (Participant 28).

To get a passport it's easy but to get a visa is too difficult to get visa, but to get a passport is easier. It's more difficult

because where we stay is so difficult to get a visa so if just
you're coming here with our passport I think it's better than
coming with a visa because visa is too difficult to get it, you
have to have money, much money, you know like maybe
R1000 so it's too difficult for that.... [Women] face problems of money like if there's no one helping them it's too
difficult to raise that money to come here, it's so difficult
(Participant 26).

Even participants from other countries commented that Zimbabweans
"don't travel easy to South Africa" (Participant 35). Aside from cost, the
limited time period permitted for stay in South Africa was described as a
further obstacle for women migrants because, as described by a long-term
migrant from Zimbabwe, "we are given short days to stay here so we are
not able to do things because our days are short here and we have to go
back home" (Participant 29).

South African Customs laws, and Customs regimes at international
borders, were also viewed as an obstacle for women migrants in the
region, and in particular those conducting cross-border trade. Difficulties
experienced with South African Customs authorities were twofold:
first, participants viewed Customs charges as too expensive, particularly
for small-scale entrepreneurs and traders. Exchanging currency to pay
Customs duties also reduces profits for cross-border traders, as described
by a short-term migrant from Zimbabwe:

Yes, they get problems at the border, they charge much
money, so the border wants so me rands and these days
when you go home I keep R100, if I come back R50 the
border charge you R300 or R150, or you got R100. So if
you don't have money they take the stuff. So it's a problem
(Participant 48).

Second, other problems emerging in interview texts were related to
goods that were confiscated, destroyed or, according to some participants,
stolen by Customs officials "for themselves."

Sometimes at the border gate they don't want us to take out
fish oil because they say fish oil is available in our countries
but it is expensive, even sugar is expensive, but they don't
want that at the border gate. Sometimes they spill it on
the ground or sometimes they take that for themselves but
they don't know how did we get money here or how did we
work hard for it, they just take. It is not the same with man
because they can fight for themselves but us woman we
won't fight back (Participant 9).

It's difficult. Because at the border I heard that they are taking everything, they are throwing everything away (Participant 47).

It's easy to travel or to trade in another country but only the rules that doesn't comply with our needs but it becomes difficult if you are carrying one bag, they search it to see what you are taking, so pay this and those are regulations that only comply and being some of our things been taken by the Customs people because they will be failing to get the foreign currency for declaration. So instead to keep the things or the goods that you go and find money to collect your things, instead they take the things wherever, you will never get them back (Participant 68).

However, it was not always clear from interview texts whether participants viewed Customs law around the declaration of goods and payment of duties as problematic for women migrants, or whether problems with Customs authorities were related to corruption or wrongdoing on the part of officials.

POLICY RECOMMENDATIONS TO BENEFIT WOMEN MIGRANTS

MVP participants were therefore asked about potential policy changes and recommendations that could make migration easier for women in the SADC region. Dodson (2000) suggests that facilitating women's migration in the region may lead to "aiding women's empowerment and allowing them to become agents of development," and adds that while it should not be unrestricted, "controlled female migration, particularly that of a short-term nature, can be harnessed as a powerful force for regional development."[44]

The majority suggested that women migrants would benefit from policies promoting freer movement and reducing restrictions on travel. Some emphasized that government should make it "easy to come here [to South Africa] and when we go back" (Participant 3), and also that "government should help by not having too much laws for women to travel, so ... that it would not be so difficult" (Participant 49).

Speaking specifically to the role of individual SADC countries in managing migration, a number of participants proposed that as a first measure, governments should come together to "talk things out" and "amend their laws" in order to facilitate easier movement across borders. Participants viewed relations between South Africa and Zimbabwe as negatively impacting on women migrants traveling between the two countries:

Just talking with the government of South Africa and
Zimbabwe for them to understand each other that will make
us come from Zimbabwe to South Africa freely. Because
what makes things difficult is that the government of South
Africa and Zimbabwe don't click. They don't listen to each
other. There is nothing that they have done. What is needed
is what they should do maybe talk things out. Things like
visas shouldn't be here I think that is the best. The changes
are not too much. The only thing that the government
should change are visa and there are no other thing that
should be changed. Yes, the rules are fine that when a person comes from Zimbabwe, should have the right documents
(Participant 28).

I think that the South African and the Zimbabwean government can meet and discuss about this visa issues because
without the visa you can't go anywhere, and we are not
comfortable to do something illegal. I think if they can discuss about cancelling the visa, things might be better for us
(Participant 46).

Participants from several countries also expressed a sense of injustice
related to differing migration regimes in individual SADC countries. In
particular, migrants commented on the difficulties Zimbabwean women
faced in traveling to South Africa, including the need to obtain expensive visas and receiving limited periods of stay in South Africa:

For business it is okay, the only thing I can say it's difficult
to migrate in Africa, it's like people like Zimbabweans, they
don't travel easy to South Africa because they must have
visas you see, but to us you travel, every time you want to
come you come.... I think they should amend their laws
that says you know, who are free to come any time here and,
because they are people and I don't know what is the problem with the Zimbabweans, you see for them to make the
visas. Because we are all the same. What is the difference
between us because they are good people in Zimbabwe and
they are bad people in Botswana as in Zimbabwe, you see its
fifty-fifty (Participant 35).

If they can cancel the visa so that all of us who come from
outside the country can use passport only, not visas, because
it is hard to get a visa...[The governments] can talk man-
to-man and end what needs to be ended like in Botswana,
we go there without visas.... They can talk about visas, and

each one of us must have a straight passport, because the passport is needed (Participant 23).

Migrants from countries such as Malawi and Lesotho also called for inter-governmental discussions, primarily related to migration push factors such as poverty, food insecurity and "suffering at home."

> Mbeki must talk to our president and discuss what should
> be done like the president of Maputo, he came and talked
> to our president that in Malawi there should not be visas. In
> Malawi the food is not like in Maputo, Bhere or Nyambane,
> it is a long distance, some things are not the same, that
> is why they have to talk so that other people don't come
> through the bushes and die because of crocodiles.... I would
> like to ask President Mbeki and the president of Malawi to
> sit down and talk about this and about how can they help us
> (Participant 9).

Participants viewed inter-governmental discussions and agreements as a strategy to improve conditions of travel and accessibility to countries in the region for women migrants; this would mean governments "should sit down as Southern Africa and talk about ladies" (Participant 34).

In terms of more specific policy recommendations, a number of participants proposed that borders to South Africa should be "opened" altogether. One migrant from Lesotho, for example, suggested that travel into South Africa should be completely unrestricted:

> My opinion is that it could be one thing – when you want
> to cross easily from any country...maybe on the border gates
> we can go willingly, as if they're opened for us, as if is one
> thing, you see (Participant 4).

Several others calling for "open" borders thought that migrants should be allowed to enter South Africa more freely and at a lesser cost. They also recommended that migrants only be required to produce an identity document, rather than a passport:

> They make it easy, but then I would like them to stop
> requiring that we should have passports so that we can trav-
> el easy and be free to come in here, and at least only need
> the ID documents to show that you are from Lesotho....
> I think that if they can cancel the passports and welcome
> everyone who's from Lesotho to South Africa and vice versa
> (Participant 5).

> Since we are struggling, when we have to go home, they
> must do that when we arrive at the border gate we must

not pay, and they make us documents allowing us to just pass through, so that we're allowed to come to South Africa (Participant 3).

The South African Immigration Amendment Act of 2004 effectively counters this suggestion by requiring nationals from neighbouring countries to possess a passport in order to qualify for a Cross-Border permit, whereas previously only an identity document was required.

A large number of participants felt that visas should be "stopped," "scrapped," or "cancelled" altogether:

> It is important for women to migrate easily because it's easy to move from one place to another after you have to stay here maybe for like a year, before you go home to see the kids, if there wasn't the issue of visas. I think people would visit their families almost every day and I think again maybe people wouldn't stay in South Africa maybe for a long time, because if they will be free to come here once they'll be given limited days at the immigration there ... with issues like visas I think it's pulling both countries backwards (Participant 19).

> I think they should discontinue the use of visa that a person who has only a passport should be allowed in Botswana for her to buy thing and be allowed in South Africa to buy things because she is doing business.... Because when I'm at home poor, not having anything and the children are crying, I would also wish to go where women go. I have to have passport and a visa to cross the border gate (Participant 32).

> If they can come here with passport they come, they buy things, they go there, they sell their goods, whatever it is, I think its better because that's the only way they can do, especially women.... I think if they can come here without using a visa I think it can be easier for them so that they can manage to come here without visa, using their own passport.... I think something important is that if they can allow people to come here without visas you know I think that the best because most of the woman, they come here for business, they go back to their country to sell their goods and everything so it's so difficult for someone with a visa to come here, you know I think that's all (Participant 26).

> The government, I can't say the government have to change, but I think it can make it easy for people, for coun-

tries such as Zimbabwe where there is hunger, no money, so you are forced to have a visa while you don't have that money, I think cause is a close country like South Africa, I think they can make it people not to use visa, just to use a passport. I believe many people here they don't come and stay, they make business and go back, so for them to have visas every time, they don't (Participant 50).

As an alternative to eliminating visas altogether, participants recommended a number of changes to visa-related restrictions, particularly for those who cross borders frequently and engage in small business and trade:

For now it is hard because I have to go in and out. This doesn't excite me because the laws of migration says we have to enter this country with a visa, if it could be like in Botswana where we don't use the visa but now the visa in Zimbabwe is too expensive to put service. And after putting the service we enter with the visa and we are given short days to stay here so we are not able to do things because our days are short here and we have to back home.... They should increase the number of days, At least if they can give us three month in South Africa it would be better because within three months you can be able to come up with something then you can go back home (Participant 29).

I think they must allow people to come as they please without the visas but hence a limited period of time like in Botswana, if you go to Botswana and you are from Zimbabwe but you are given 30 days, like 90 days for the whole year. In that year maybe you are not allowed to go back into the country maybe for about 5 years. You see if you are in Zimbabwe within those 10 days make sure you go back home because you don't want you passport taken away from you. So I think if the government does something I think many people including me maybe I can go back home (Participant 19).

The notion of less restricted movement across regional borders is in line with the provisions of the Draft SADC Protocol on the Facilitation of Free Movement of Persons, which would allow visa-free entry temporary visitors into participating states for up to 90 days.[45]

Beyond issues of the accessibility of South Africa to migrants from other countries, participants called for a number of other improvements to the migration regime. First, although many demonstrated an awareness of law and policy, participants called for greater access to information for migrants themselves. A number felt more information should be available at border posts. A number of participants also suggested that governments in the region should increase accessibility to travel documents for women migrants. More specifically in South Africa, participants felt migrant women should be provided with IDs, in order to access a number of services, such as schools, bank accounts and housing:

> We women have a lot of ideas that we want to implement but we can't. For example, if I had my ID document, I wouldn't stay at the flat, but I would have done all this in my own house, I prefer to have my own house but I can't do that because I don't have the necessary document (Participant 11).

> When we stay here for more than eight years they are supposed to give us like a temporary ID so that we can stay here nicely because we are employing people from here in South Africa. Like me I have employed two people from here in South Africa...By now you can see they are helping us, but we are facing many problems. Like when we want to buy something they refuse to sell it to us because we are foreigners, they can't take credit from the furniture shop because we don't have IDs. We can't open an account at the bank because we don't have IDs (Short Malawi 24).

> If we don't have South African IDs, we are unable to open up bank accounts or buy anything because of an ID. So the government can help on such situation (Participant 42).

As many participants migrated to South Africa looking for work or other economic opportunities, they suggested that having IDs and other "legal papers" would help them to find jobs and enter into employment. IDs were also suggested as a means to avoid harassment by the police. A migrant from Mozambique also pointed out that providing non-citizens with IDs would allow the South African government to differentiate between legal migrants, and those who were not. She explained that having an ID is "good because they arrest you in order to have an ID that identify you and shows where you come from so that when you've done something wrong they are able to find you."

An additional policy recommendation voiced by cross-border traders was that customs laws and policies should be amended to be more accommodating for women migrants conducting small-scale business and shopping. A number felt that export duties are too expensive and should be reduced or eliminated altogether:

Officials at the border are friendly, but the export duty laws for cars and other things that you are carrying are costly. I think that they should be ignored. They should cancel that law, people shouldn't pay the export duty (Participant 2).

Yes, there at the border I can say it is too tough when we cross the border with the stuff like outside stuff, which we sell here in South Africa. It is too tough because other people, they just come with the stuff without paying for it. But if they got permit they are going to pass nicely at the border. And also people at the border must think about us like the price they are over-charging (Participant 39).

I think that if they can make it simple for us, because sometimes they charge us duties for our things at the border gate and we sometimes don't have enough money because we don't know how much they would want ... when we are from home we bring some things to sell, so don't know how much are we going to pay for those things at the border gate, we only get the price when we arrive there. They sometimes charge us a lot, it depends. We are not refusing to pay but they should charge us reasonably (Participant 46).

If the traveling cost rates can be reduced. When you sell things like calabash for R5 then when you go home all the money is spend on transport then you are left with no profit. If they can try to think for hawkers, especially in the border post to reduce tax, if you are registered and sell legally, not those who sell drugs because they destroy the nation. But people who sell things like handicraft are good (Participant 16).

Focusing on the conditions under which women migrants travel, participants suggested that governments should also put more measures in place to combat crime and improve levels of "protection, safety and security":

Yes, the problem they experience normally is not having confidence that they are safe when they travel ... a woman can need help by increasing security and for a woman to feel safe when she travel to South Africa from other countries for her not to have fear especially when she travels at night, because a person is not restricted when to travel. Protection must be there (Participant 64).

> It will be the same only the thing that he will be worried about are tsotsis, who steals men's goods and women's goods so mostly we could as for the security to look after that, but at the moment now security is robbing some of our women (Participant 68).

Participants also said that measures could be taken to improve the quality of cross-border transportation:

> At least, they should subsidize the transport to be much cheaper and they should provide security that will patrol around us, so that we would feel safe wherever we go (Participant 5).

> The problem is that I used a train before so now I haven't used a train in a long time, it was better on the train because it was taking us out of here and we didn't pay but now things are expensive and the prices have gone up.... [The governments] should sit and talk so that we can be able to help our children. At least the train is not making us to pay more, even the buses they should not charge a lot because money is scarce these days (Participant 9).

Finally, underscoring the difficulties they face in their interactions with citizens and government, several participants appealed for better treatment of women migrants in South Africa:

> The government can help us by appreciating us in the country and treat us the same with the other people in South Africa (Participant 45).

> I would like to say if people can change and treat other people from other country in a way that they are people, 'cause I believe no one can want to leave his country without nothing, so what makes people to come here is because the situation is bad, so I think if people can just try to live with people in a good way (Participant 50).

> I think women should get proper treatment. When they are in South Africa they must be free and treated better when going back home. At the border there the Customs officers at the border must know that these people went to South Africa, not for enjoyment but because of the suffering they are going through. The way women are treated is bad (Participant 73).

CONCLUSION

National immigration statistics indicate that women traveling through formal channels have been migrating in and out of South Africa at a rate nearly on par with that of male migrants across the latter half of the past century. However, little research has been conducted thus far on the experiences of women migrants in the region, which as in other parts of the world has been linked to the "near invisibility of women as migrants, their presumed passivity in the migration process, and their assumed place in the home."[46] Rather than as independent migrants themselves, women in Southern Africa in particular have instead been construed as those who are "left behind," and as "'passive rural widows' who stayed put somewhere, practicing subsistence, and later, cash crop agricultural production while their men departed, perhaps never to return."[47]

In-depth interviews conducted through the Migrant Voices Project uncovered the stories and experiences of a group of Southern African migrant women who were far from "passive rural widows." On the contrary, most of the migrant women participating in the project were main household breadwinners who left the countries of origin seeking an economic livelihood to support themselves and their children, as well as elderly parents, siblings, and extended family members.

The findings of the Migrant Voices Project confirmed some well-researched features of migration in the Southern Africa region. Poverty has been, and continues to be, a foremost determining "push factor" in both individual and household decision-making processes that lead to migration, and is also interlinked to high levels of unemployment, currency inflation, natural disasters such as drought, and food insecurity in SADC countries. Participants generally viewed South Africa as the most affluent country in the region, and with the widest range of economic opportunities on offer, although South African women also cited pursuit of jobs and other economic opportunities as reasons for migrating elsewhere. A deeply gendered dimension of the relationship between poverty and migration that emerged from interview texts was the often singular responsibility women assumed in providing for households and children, resulting from both relationship breakdowns, and the unwillingness of male partners to contribute towards family expenses. Women's migration decisions were therefore often tinged by a profound sense of both obligation and urgency. This raises questions about gendered productive roles within families in the SADC region, and perhaps specifically within migrant-sending households, as a possible site for future research.

Consistent with the findings of earlier SAMP research, women participants were discouraged from migrating by families or community members in a number of cases. However, interview texts suggest that this discouragement was generally linked to fears about vulnerability to abuse and crime while traveling or living in a foreign country, more so than for reasons related to subverting traditional gender roles locating women with children and in the home. Accordingly, women were almost always received positively when returning home to families and communities, and did not appear to suffer negative social consequences as a result of migrating. At the same time, Migrant Voices research was clearly unable to reach women in the region who may have been so strongly discouraged that they chose not to migrate.

Migrant Voices also confirmed that, as recognized in the global context by the GCIM in 2005, migration "can be an empowering experience for women." Most research felt they had benefited from exposure to different languages and cultures, greater access to commercial and "lifestyle" goods such as clothing and electronic equipment, and a sense of independence and freedom. Women also found that their individual economic circumstances improved after migrating. While for some new income allowed for little more than basic survival, other migrants were ultimately able to invest new income into purchasing businesses, cars and houses.

Migrant-sending households were in fact more significant beneficiaries of migration than individual women themselves. In most cases, women described spending new income on food, clothing and toiletries for family left behind in countries of origin, as well as remitting cash on a regular basis. Many women also invested new income in education, paying for school fees for their children as well as siblings and other family members in countries of origin. Significantly, this suggests that amongst the women interviewed, migration has led to poverty alleviation at the household level, and to investment in social goods and services.

Interview texts also underscored a number of extremely negative features of migration for women in the SADC region. While participants who travelled legally through established border posts described relatively few problems, women who "jumped the fence" faced a barrage of risks and rights abuses. These included arduous journeys through "the bush" at night, constant fear of being detected by police or Immigration officials, fear of attacks by wild animals, and abuse and abandonment at the hands of paid guides. Women who were caught crossing borders illegally by police, security or Immigration officials also described being solicited for bribes and sex in exchange for entry into South Africa. As told by a Focus Group participant who was caught close to the Beitbridge border, "I slept with the soldiers because I didn't even have a single cent." Women migrants who are faced with poverty in countries of origin, are responsible for household livelihoods, and view travel documentation as expensive and unattainable, will likely continue to face inhumane abuse of this kind when traveling through irregular means.

Consistent with previous SAMP research documenting high levels of xenophobia in South Africa, most migrant women faced little or no prospect of social integration in the country, and were confronted with exclusion, harassment, and even abuse on a daily basis. The most frequent manifestation of deep-seated xenophobia was regular name-calling, a source of shock, anger and humiliation for many women migrants. A migrant from Lesotho told SAMP that South African citizens "treat you like dogs" with "no right to be here." Migrant women also felt that non-citizens are often depicted as "desperate and poor," and are blamed for crime, taking jobs from South Africans, and "stealing husbands."

In response, women developed a number of coping strategies, which included efforts to speak in local dialects, "learn South African culture," adopt local clothing styles, and generally to "disguise that you are a foreigner." Women also sought to live and work in areas populated by other non-citizens, such as Hillbrow in downtown Johannesburg. Many women seeking partners or spouses while in South Africa also preferred relationships with foreign men, whom they viewed as more understanding of responsibilities towards children and families in countries of origin, less likely to impose strict social "rules" that would be difficult to understand, and ultimately, less xenophobic.

Women were also excluded from access to a number of critical basic services in South Africa. Although the Constitution guarantees "equal protection and benefit of the law" for all persons within the country, migrant women were regularly harassed and solicited for bribes by SAPS and Metro police officers, who were also reported to regularly destroy passports and IDs without differentiation between legal and fraudulent documents. Distrust of the police, and fear of arrest and deportation, meant women migrants were effectively excluded from legal protection in South Africa. Further, women who were arrested and sent to Lindela Repatriation Centre stated that they had been solicited by officers for cash bribes and sex, experienced beatings and physical abuse, were denied food and adequate blankets, and were detained in unhygienic conditions. These experiences are a direct contravention of the Minimum Standards of Detention prescribed by the Department of Home Affairs in the Immigration Regulations of 2005.[48]

A second major point of exclusion was from medical services and health care, as has been documented in several previous studies in South Africa.[49] This is in spite of international recognition of the "complex" health care needs of women migrants, which include risks related to vulnerability to HIV and other STI's, limited access to contraceptives, violence and sexual abuse, and the difficulty of "safe motherhood."[50]

Participants described being called derogatory names and refused services by health professionals, most commonly when seeking prenatal care or when giving birth, again despite the Constitutional right of "access to health care services, including reproductive health care" and the guarantee that "no one may be refused emergency medical treatment."[51] Women told SAMP that they had given birth in South African hospitals with little or no assistance from medical professionals, at great risk to their own health and that of their children.

Overall, these findings support and underscore the results of a number of previous studies, and suggest that the experiences of migrant women living in South Africa are often characterized by exclusion, fear and insecurity, in spite of the positive individual and economic changes many experience.

At the same time, texts from in-depth interviews and focus groups revealed a number of relatively new findings with relation to women's migration experiences in the SADC region. First, there was strong consensus amongst participants that migration is important for women in the SADC region. Although the value of migration was crucially linked to access to economic opportunity, women also discussed the importance of travel "for travel's sake," including the social and intellectual benefits of exposure to different cultures and environments and greater access to opportunities for skills development and education. These benefits are often recognized in the context of tourism and foreign study, but overlooked in relation to poor migrants.

In spite of the hardships experienced by participants, from leaving family behind in countries of origin to dangerous travel conditions and exclusion and xenophobia in South Africa, many felt that migration was generally "easy" for women in the SADC region. In fact, many participants viewed migration as "easier" for women than for men, in spite of obstacles such as vulnerability to abuse and harassment, a lack of social "power" and limited access to the financial means necessary for travel. "Easier" migration for women was attributed to a number of gendered characteristics, including inherent qualities of trustworthiness, honesty and likeability; the ability to "talk" or "speak," particularly to authority figures such as Immigration officers; and, the advantage of a stronger emotional and intellectual link to families and children in countries of origin. Women did, however, view male migrants as advantaged by higher levels of education, better access to jobs, and lesser financial obligation towards family and children in countries of origin.

Most women, including both "legal" and "illegal" migrants, had a working understanding of the requirements of South African immigration law and policy, based on their own travel experiences as well as information from other migrants, the media, border posts, and government offices. Women viewed migration as "easier" for migrants who "have the correct papers and "obey the rules," and viewed legal migration as the "safe" and "right" way to travel. Interview texts also suggested that women respect the right of South Africa and other states in the region to determine and enforce migration law and policy. As also found in Dodson's (1998) analysis, these findings suggest that women migrants are generally "law-abiding" and may "have a higher incidence of legal migration than male migrants."[52] However, for some women migrants the cost associated with legal travel, including visas and the requirement of "sufficient available funds," remain prohibitively high. These costs were viewed as having a disproportionately negative effect on poor women, on cross-border traders wishing travel frequently for short periods of time, and in particular, Zimbabwean migrants. Further, these costs appeared to lead directly to decisions to migrate through "the border-jumping method," rather than prevent poor migrants from entering South Africa.

Beyond these findings, the Migrant Voices Project also gave participants the opportunity to discuss potential changes to migration policy in South Africa and the SADC region that they felt would benefit other women migrants. First, with notable congruence to the re-emergence of regional debate around the SADC Protocol on the Facilitation of Free Movement of Persons[53], many women migrants called for fundamentally fewer restrictions on travel across the region. As a starting point, they proposed meetings between national governments in the region to "talk things out" and "amend their laws" in order to: address push factors such as poverty and food insecurity, harmonize migration policy and introduce "laws which are friendly to foreigners," and facilitate freer migration. Interstate relations between South Africa and Zimbabwe in particular were viewed as impacting negatively on women's migration, with participants observing that the two governments "don't click" and "don't listen to each other." However, the call for improved inter-state communication and cooperation on issues of migration was extended to include many other governments in the region in addition to Zimbabwe and South Africa, such as Lesotho, Malawi and Mozambique.

Beyond the proposal that SADC states should generally strengthen communication and inter-governmental relations in order to move towards freer movement in the region, participants made a number of specific suggestions for removing migration restrictions. These included calls for completely "open" borders, as well as more moderate suggestions of reduced visa and Customs costs, more flexible time periods for stay in South Africa, and the ability for migrants to travel within SADC using only IDs, rather than passports. There was also enormous support amongst participants for the "scrapping" of visas required to enter South Africa, and here, many migrants expressed a willingness to obtain passports and travel with legal documentation as long as visas are not required. Women emphasized difficulties experienced by cross-border traders who "don't come [to South Africa] and stay, they make business and go back," but must undergo a costly visa application process prior to each journey. Again, this is consistent with conditions outlined within the SADC Protocol, which proposes visa-free travel between State Parties for up to 90 days for foreign visitors, provided that migrants possess valid travel documents, provide "evidence of sufficient means of support for the duration of the visit," are not "prohibited persons" according to the laws of the host country, and cross the border through official ports of entry.[54]

Given that women migrants participating in the study wish to travel through regular and legal means, and were willing to travel with passports, eliminating visitor visa requirements for citizens of SADC countries would likely lead to more regularized travel overall. This has potential to reduce the enormous fiscal and management burdens of monitoring and controlling irregular migration for SADC states, while also improving conditions of travel for migrants in the region. For example, the South African Department of Home Affairs reports that 167,137 "illegal foreigners" were deported from South Africa in 2004, and 209,988 in 2005.[55] The majority of these "illegal foreigners" are citizens of other SADC countries. The United Nations High Commissioner for Refugees (UNHCR) in Pretoria reported that the 154,000 migrants detained at the Lindela Repatriation Centre during 2003 included the following approximate number of SADC country nationals: 82,000 from Mozambique; 55,000 from Zimbabwe; 7000 from Lesotho; 4700 from Malawi; and 1000 each from Tanzania and Swaziland.[56] The cost of removals and deportations during 2005 was estimated at R200 million,[57] and the costs of operating the Lindela Centre are "reported to be twice those of a normal South African prison."[58]

Introducing visa-free travel for temporary visitors, however, would not specifically address the needs of cross-border traders, who would benefit from less restrictive entry requirements in South African but would still not have the right to legal trade or business. Creating a specific visa for small-scale traders and entrepreneurs to conduct business in South Africa, or even in countries across the entire region, would support SADC's goals of achieving regional economic integration and cooperation, and enhance the anti-poverty and developmental migration outcomes that women participants described, such as greater household income, food security and investment in education.

The participants also identified a range of services that would benefit women migrants, beginning with more accessible information about migration laws and policy. Many viewed it as important for migrants to have some form of identity document that would allow access to certain critical services, such as the ability to enrol children in schools, open bank accounts, obtain credit, enter into accommodation lease agreements, and to purchase a home or other property. The participants also suggested that providing legal migrants with recognized identity documents would reduce instances of police harassment and abuse, while also allowing for better differentiation between legal and illegal migrants.[59] Currently, South African national identity documents are only available to citizens and permanent residents, and separate documents are issued to recognized refugees.

Participants suggested that women in the region require far greater protection when migrating, in a number of different respects. Women called for more security to combat crime around border areas, as well as safer transport and accommodation. Finally, reflecting negative experiences in interacting with citizens and government, participants appealed for the equal treatment of migrants in South Africa.

ENDNOTES

1   Nancy Yinger, "The Feminization of Migration" Population Reference Bureau, Washington, 2006; Aderanti Adepoju, "Changing Configurations of Migration in Africa" Migration Information Source, Migration Policy Institute, 2004; Gloria Moreno Fontes Chammartin, "The Feminization of International Migration" International Labour Organization, 2005; International Organization for Migration (IOM), *International Migration Law: Glossary on Migration* (Geneva: International Organization for Migration, 2005).

2   Hania Zlotnik, "The Global Dimensions of Female Migration" Migration Information Source, Migration Policy Institute, 2003.

3   Ibid.

4   Hania Zlotnik, "International Migration in Africa: An Analysis Based on Estimates of the Migrant Stock" Migration Information Source, Migration Policy Institute, 2003.

5   G. Hugo, *Migration and Development: A Perspective from Asia.* IOM Migration Research Series 14, Geneva, 2003.

6   United Nations Department of Economic and Social Affairs: Division for the Advancement of Women, *2004 World Survey on the Role of Women in Development: Women and International Migration* (New York: United Nations, 2005), p. 11.

7   Robin Cohen, "International Migration: Southern Africa in Global Perspective", in Jonathan Crush and F. Veriava, *Transforming South African Immigration Policy: Papers for the Green Paper on International Migration Task Team* (Cape Town: SAMP, 1997).

8   Monica Boyd and Elizabeth Grieco, "Women and Migration: Incorporating Gender into International Migration Theory" Migration Information Source, Migration Policy Institute, 2003.

9   Belinda Dodson and Jonathan Crush, "Report on Gender Discrimination in South Africa's 2002 Immigration Act: Masculinizing the Migrant", *Feminist Review* 77(2004): 96-119.

10 Teresa A. Barnes, *"We Women Worked so Hard": Gender, Urbanization and Social Reproduction in Colonial Harare, Zimbabwe, 1930-1956* (Portsmouth NH: Heinemann, 1999); Belinda Bozzoli and Mmantho Nkotsoe, *Women of Phokeng: Consciousness, Life Strategy and Migrancy in South Africa, 1900-83* (Portsmouth NH: Heinemann, 1991).

11 Alan Jeeves and Jonathan Crush (eds.), *White Farms, Black Labor: The State and Agrarian Change in Southern Africa, 1910-1950* (Pietermaritzburg: University of Natal Press, 1997).

12 Camilla Cockerton, "Running Away from 'The Land of the Desert': Women's Migration from Colonial Botswana to South Africa, c. 1895-1966", unpublished PhD thesis, Queen's University, Kingston, Ontario, 1995; Hamilton Simelane, "The State, Chiefs and the Control of Female Migration in Colonial Swaziland, c. 1930s-1950s", *Journal of African History* 45 (2004): 103-24.

13 Philip Bonner, "Desirable or undesirable Basotho women? Liquor, prostitution and the migration of Basotho women to the Rand, 1920-1945", in C. Walker (ed), *Women and Gender in Southern Africa to 1945* (Cape Town: David Philip and London: James Currey, 1990); M Miles, "Missing Women: A Study of Swazi Female Migration to the Witwatersrand 1920-1970", unpublished MA thesis, Queen's University, Kingston, Ontario, 1991; Cockerton, "Running Away from 'The Land of the Desert'".

14 Dodson and Crush, "Gender Discrimination in South Africa's 2002 Immigration Act".

15 Wade Pendleton, Jonathan Crush, Eugene Campbell, Thuso Green, Hamilton Simelane, Daniel Tevera and Fion de Vletter, *Migration, Remittances and Development in Southern Africa*, Migration Policy Series No. 44, SAMP, 2006.

16 Belinda Dodson, *Women on the Move: Gender and Cross-Border Migration to South Africa*, Migration Policy Series No. 9, SAMP, 1998.

17 Boyd and Grieco, "Women and Migration".

18 Dodson, *Women on the Move*, p. 19.

19 Vincent Williams and Lizzie Carr, "The Draft Protocol on the Facilitation of Movement of Persons in SADC: Implications for State Parties", Migration Policy Brief No. 18, SAMP, 2006.

20 Dodson and Crush, "Gender Discrimination in South Africa's 2002 Immigration Act."

21 Global Commission on International Migration (GCIM), "Migration in an Interconnected World: New Directions for Action", 2005, p. 49.

22 Dodson and Crush, "Gender Discrimination in South Africa's 2002 Immigration Act".

23 Belinda Dodson, "Women on the Move: Gender and Cross-Border Migration to South Africa from Lesotho, Mozambique and Zimbabwe", in David A. McDonald (ed.), *On Borders: Perspectives on International Migration in Southern Africa* (Cape Town: SAMP, 2000), p. 133.

24 Dodson, *Women on the Move*, p. 19.

25 Dodson and Crush, "Gender Discrimination in South Africa's 2002 Immigration Act".

26 Dodson, *Women on the Move*, p. 20.

27 Ibid., p. 135.

28 Mary J. Osirim, "African Women's Entrepreneurship and Cultural Production: The Case of Crocheters and Knitters in Southern Africa", *Contours: A Journal of the African Diaspora* 1(2) (Fall 2003): p. 154.

29 Dodson, *Women on the Move*, p. 25.

30 Unity Chari, "Informal Cross Border Trade and Gender" Presentation at the Workshop on Sustainable Development Through Trade, 2004, at *www.zero.org.zw/networks/docs/Trade%20and%20Gender.pdf*.

31 See Lisa Daniels, "Changes in the Small-Scale Enterprise Sector from 1991

to 1993: Results of a Second Nationwide Survey in Zimbabwe", Gemini Technical Report No. 71, March 1994, p. 30, in *Structural Adjustment and Women Informal Sector Traders in Harare, Zimbabwe*. Sweden: Nordiska Afrikainstitutet, p. 16.

32 Jonathan Crush, *Immigration, Xenophobia and Human Rights in South Africa*, Migration Policy Series No. 22, SAMP and South African Human Rights Commission, 2001, pp. 2-3.

33 "Speech By The Minister Of Home Affairs, MS N.N. Mapisa-Nqakula, MP, Introducing The Immigration Amendment Bill, 2004, to the National Assembly On 19 August 2004".

34 David A. McDonald and Sean Jacobs, *Understanding Press Coverage of Cross-Border Migration in Southern Africa Since 2000*, Migration Policy Series No. 37, SAMP, 2005, pp. 1-2; Ransford Danso and David A. McDonald, *Writing Xenophobia: Immigration and the Press in Post-Apartheid South Africa*, Migration Policy Series No. 17, SAMP, 2000.

35 See Department of Home Affairs, "Immigration Act 2002: Immigration Regulations", June 2005.

36 South African Broadcasting Corporation (SABC) "Room A6", Special Assignment, September 6, 2005.

37 Ibid.

38 Department of Home Affairs, "Ministerial Committee of Enquiry into Recent Deaths at Lindela Holding Facility," 2005, p. 7.

39 Ibid., p. 10. See also "Refugee Rights Project Detention Monitoring," Lawyers for Human Rights, August 2005; "Lindela at Crossroads for Detention and Repatriation", Human Rights Commission, 12 December 2000; "Report into Arrest and Detention of Suspected Undocumented Migrants," South African Human Rights Commission, 19 March 1999.

40 Department of Home Affairs, "Ministerial Committee of Enquiry", p. 9.

41 Ibid., pp. 6-7.

42 See, for example, Dunbar Moodie, "Town Women and Country Wives: Housing Preferences at Vaal Reefs Mine", in Jonathan Crush and Wilmot James (eds.), *Crossing Boundaries: Mine Migrancy in a Democratic South Africa* (Cape Town: IDASA/IDRC, 1995), pp. 68-81; Jonathan Crush, "Migrations Past: An Historical Overview of Cross-Border Movement in Southern Africa" in McDonald, *On Borders*, pp. 12-24.

43 Republic of South Africa, "Immigration Amendment Act, 2004", *Government Gazette*, Vol. 472, No. 26901 (18 October 2004), Sec. 13 (a).

44 Dodson, *Women on the Move*, p. 44.

45 See *SADC Draft Protocol on the Facilitation of Movement of Persons*, Article 14.

46 Boyd and Grieco, "Women and Migration".

47 C Murray, *Families Divided: The Impact of Migrant Labour in Lesotho* (Cambridge: Cambridge University Press, 1981).

48 Department of Home Affairs, "Ministerial Committee of Enquiry".

49   See Sally Peberdy, Jonathan Crush and Ntombikayise Msibi, "Migrants in the City of Johannesburg: A Report for the City of Johannesburg" SAMP, 2004; Community Agency for Social Enquiry (CASE), *National Refugee Baseline Survey: Final Report* (Pretoria: Capture Press, 2003); Zonke Majodina and Sally Peberdy, with the Somali Association of South Africa, "Finding a New Home: A Report on the Lives of Somali Refugees in Johannesburg", Forced Migration Studies Programme, University of the Witwatersrand, August 2000.

50   See United Nations Department of Economic and Social Affairs: Division for the Advancement of Women, 2005; "People Who Move: New Reproductive Health Focus", *Population Reports*, 24.n3 (November 1996): 1(27).

51   Constitution of the Republic of South Africa, Ch. 2.27.1-3.

52   Dodson, *Women on the Move*, pp. 20, 30.

53   See, for example, Beauregard Tromp, "SADC nations pledge to market the region", *The Star*, 19 August 2005, p. 5.

54   *SADC Draft Protocol.*

55   Department of Home Affairs, "Annual Report 2005-2006" Pretoria, 2006, p. 22.

56   O. Field, "Alternatives to Detention of Asylum-Seekers and Refugees", *Legal and Protection Policy Research Series*. Geneva: United Nations High Commissioner for Refugees, Division of International Protection Services, 2006, p. 178.

57   E. Naidu, "When a Life of Hell is Better than Home", *Sunday Independent*, 13 August 2006.

58   F. Jenkins, F and L.A. de la Hunt, "Detaining Asylum-Seekers: Perspectives on Reception Centres for Asylum Seekers in South Africa", University of Cape Town Legal Aid Clinic, September 2000, p. 4.

59   See also C Mini, "Register Foreigners Living in South Africa, for Our Own Peace of Mind", *Sunday Times*, 16 July 2006.

MIGRATION POLICY SERIES

1. *Covert Operations: Clandestine Migration, Temporary Work and Immigration Policy in South Africa* (1997) ISBN 1-874864-51-9
2. *Riding the Tiger: Lesotho Miners and Permanent Residence in South Africa* (1997) ISBN 1-874864-52-7
3. *International Migration, Immigrant Entrepreneurs and South Africa's Small Enterprise Economy* (1997) ISBN 1-874864-62-4
4. *Silenced by Nation Building: African Immigrants and Language Policy in the New South Africa* (1998) ISBN 1-874864-64-0
5. *Left Out in the Cold? Housing and Immigration in the New South Africa* (1998) ISBN 1-874864-68-3
6. *Trading Places: Cross-Border Traders and the South African Informal Sector* (1998) ISBN 1-874864-71-3
7. *Challenging Xenophobia: Myth and Realities about Cross-Border Migration in Southern Africa* (1998) ISBN 1-874864-70-5
8. *Sons of Mozambique: Mozambican Miners and Post-Apartheid South Africa* (1998) ISBN 1-874864-78-0
9. *Women on the Move: Gender and Cross-Border Migration to South Africa* (1998) ISBN 1-874864-82-9.
10. *Namibians on South Africa: Attitudes Towards Cross-Border Migration and Immigration Policy* (1998) ISBN 1-874864-84-5.
11. *Building Skills: Cross-Border Migrants and the South African Construction Industry* (1999) ISBN 1-874864-84-5
12. *Immigration & Education: International Students at South African Universities and Technikons* (1999) ISBN 1-874864-89-6
13. *The Lives and Times of African Immigrants in Post-Apartheid South Africa* (1999) ISBN 1-874864-91-8
14. *Still Waiting for the Barbarians: South African Attitudes to Immigrants and Immigration* (1999) ISBN 1-874864-91-8
15. *Undermining Labour: Migrancy and Sub-contracting in the South African Gold Mining Industry* (1999) ISBN 1-874864-91-8
16. *Borderline Farming: Foreign Migrants in South African Commercial Agriculture* (2000) ISBN 1-874864-97-7
17. *Writing Xenophobia: Immigration and the Press in Post-Apartheid South Africa* (2000) ISBN 1-919798-01-3
18. *Losing Our Minds: Skills Migration and the South African Brain Drain* (2000) ISBN 1-919798-03-x
19. *Botswana: Migration Perspectives and Prospects* (2000) ISBN 1-919798-04-8
20. *The Brain Gain: Skilled Migrants and Immigration Policy in Post-Apartheid South Africa* (2000) ISBN 1-919798-14-5
21. *Cross-Border Raiding and Community Conflict in the Lesotho-South African Border Zone* (2001) ISBN 1-919798-16-1
22. *Immigration, Xenophobia and Human Rights in South Africa* (2001) ISBN 1-919798-30-7

23. *Gender and the Brain Drain from South Africa* (2001) ISBN 1-919798-35-8

24. *Spaces of Vulnerability: Migration and HIV/AIDS in South Africa* (2002) ISBN 1-919798-38-2

25. *Zimbabweans Who Move: Perspectives on International Migration in Zimbabwe* (2002) ISBN 1-919798-40-4

26. *The Border Within: The Future of the Lesotho-South African International Boundary* (2002) ISBN 1-919798-41-2

27. *Mobile Namibia: Migration Trends and Attitudes* (2002) ISBN 1-919798-44-7

28. *Changing Attitudes to Immigration and Refugee Policy in Botswana* (2003) ISBN 1-919798-47-1

29. *The New Brain Drain from Zimbabwe* (2003) ISBN 1-919798-48-X

30. *Regionalizing Xenophobia? Citizen Attitudes to Immigration and Refugee Policy in Southern Africa* (2004) ISBN 1-919798-53-6

31. *Migration, Sexuality and HIV/AIDS in Rural South Africa* (2004) ISBN 1-919798-63-3

32. *Swaziland Moves: Perceptions and Patterns of Modern Migration* (2004) ISBN 1-919798-67-6

33. *HIV/AIDS and Children's Migration in Southern Africa* (2004) ISBN 1-919798-70-6

34. *Medical Leave: The Exodus of Health Professionals from Zimbabwe* (2005) ISBN 1-919798-74-9

35. *Degrees of Uncertainty: Students and the Brain Drain in Southern Africa* (2005) ISBN 1-919798-84-6

36. *Restless Minds: South African Students and the Brain Drain* (2005) ISBN 1-919798-82-X

37. *Understanding Press Coverage of Cross-Border Migration in Southern Africa since 2000* (2005) ISBN 1-919798-91-9

38. *Northern Gateway: Cross-Border Migration Between Namibia and Angola* (2005) ISBN 1-919798-92-7

39. *Early Departures: The Emigration Potential of Zimbabwean Students* (2005) ISBN 1-919798-99-4

40. *Migration and Domestic Workers: Worlds of Work, Health and Mobility in Johannesburg* (2005) ISBN 1-920118-02-0

41. *The Quality of Migration Services Delivery in South Africa* (2005) ISBN 1-920118-03-9

42. *States of Vulnerability: The Future Brain Drain of Talent to South Africa* (2006) ISBN 1-920118-07-1

43. *Migration and Development in Mozambique: Poverty, Inequality and Survival* (2006) ISBN 1-920118-10-1

44. *Migration, Remittances and Development in Southern Africa* (2006) ISBN 1-920118-15-2

45. *Medical Recruiting: The Case of South African Health Care Professionals* (2007) ISBN 1-920118-47-0

www.ingramcontent.com/pod-product-compliance
Lightning Source LLC
Chambersburg PA
CBHW080001280326
41935CB00013B/1712